Content Marketing
Made Easy
Why You Need It / How to Do It

Susan Crossman

Manor House

Library and Archives Canada Cataloguing in Publication

Crossman, Susan, author
	Content marketing made easy : why you need it / how to do it / Susan Crossman.

ISBN 978-1-988058-02-3 (paperback).

--ISBN 978-1-988058-03-0 (bound)

	1. Internet marketing--Handbooks, manuals, etc.
2. Marketing--
Handbooks, manuals, etc. I. Title.

HF5415.1265.C76 2015   658.8'72
C2015-906077-X

Copyright: Susan Crossman and Manor House Publishing Inc.

Full cover design/realization Donovan Davie: 519-501-2375
Front Cover image: 'Money Icon' courtesy Shutterstock / inspiron.dell

First Edition. 240 pages. All rights reserved.
Published October 15, 2015
Manor House Publishing Inc.
www.manor-house.biz (905) 648-2193

We acknowledge the financial support of the Government of Canada through the Canada Book Fund (CBF) for this title.

For My Father, Tom Crossman, whose curiosity and imagination about almost everything helped spark in me a sense of wonder and a love of learning.

Contents

Acknowledgements 6

Introduction: Content Marketing/Social Media Context 8

Chapter 1:   Content Marketing? What Does that Mean? 15

Chapter 2:   Getting Started 22

Chapter 3:   Taking Another Step 35

Chapter 4:   We Have to Talk about Your Brand 45

Chapter 5:   Writing for the Web 56

Chapter 6:   Writing Better 73

Chapter 7:   Your Website 87

Chapter 8:   Your Blog 99

Chapter 9:   Your Company Newsletter 121

Chapter 10: Social Media Marketing (SMM) 133

Chapter 11: Email Marketing 163

Chapter 12: Online Public Relations 174

Chapter 13: Search Engine Optimization (SEO) 185

Chapter 14: Measurement 194

Chapter 15: Tools 207

Conclusion: Pulling it all Together 219

About the Author: 239

Before we get started...

Thank you for purchasing *Content Marketing Made Easy*. If you would like to download a free audio version of this book, I invite you to visit www.crossmancommunications.com/cmbookdownload to obtain access to it.

- Susan Crossman

I also invite you to take a minute and:

- Connect with me, Susan Crossman, on LinkedIn
- Follow me on Twitter (@CrossmanCom)
- Like the Crossman Communications Facebook page
- Add Susan Crossman and Crossman Communications to your circles on Google+ and/or
- If you'd like to know more about how Crossman Communications can support your content marketing objectives, contact me directly at susan@crossmancommunications.com

Acknowledgements

Writing a book is a wonderful adventure, although it can be a solitary occupation. This is especially true at 4:45 every weekday morning when I find myself hunched over my keyboard in earnest pursuit of the ideas and words that seem to be just as earnestly focused on evading capture. I chase and they flee for about an hour-and-a-half a day, for months on end, and it's with honest surprise I come to the end of the game and discover that I have written another book. Did I prevail? Or did those rascally words and ideas *willingly* submit to my efforts to organize them in an order I consider logical?

And was I really alone all those dark and quiet mornings? By the end of the project I had the company of more than 55,000 hand-picked words to cheer me on, every single one of which I met and considered, pondered and selected. Many times. In a more fanciful mood, I consider all those words (and the thousands that didn't make the final cut) to be part of my team and I thank them for their participation in this book.

An even more important part of my team, and appreciated so much, are my children, Heather Christie, Michael Quigley and Michelle Quigley, who stood by me at the announcement that another book was in the offing and encouraged me. Even when I arose every morning to crash numbly into furniture and doors in the pre-dawn darkness, and when I shattered the silence of a sleeping household with my beloved Keurig coffee maker, I was never once reproached for my lack of consideration (or my imperfect coordination). In fact, I think they are all rather proud of their mother, and I am so glad to be part of their family.

To Leah Roberts and Tania Brown, I offer my heartfelt thanks for your brilliant ideas, tireless support, endless dedication and cheerful research assistance. I'm grateful for your willingness to lend your energy to the building of the amazing company we're creating and I'm in awe of your talents and creativity.

To Barb Stuhlemmer, CEO of Blitz Business Success — your business insights and strategic input have been invaluable, and I appreciate your dedication, your wisdom, your support and, most of all, your friendship.

To Jennifer Hough, CEO of The Wide Awakening—thank you, Sistah, for teaching me so much about the importance of flow as it applies to running a business. And, in fact, as it applies to living a life. I can't imagine what my world would be like if you hadn't awakened me to so many new possibilities. Your friendship empowers and inspires me.

To Laura Gisborne, CEO of Gisborne Development—you are continually sharing new distinctions with me in the areas of business development and marketing and I appreciate so very much your guidance, your friendship and your support.

To my clients, who know who they are – I thank you for your business and your faith in me and my team. It is an honour and a delight to serve you and me and my team are grateful for the chance to be on the writing/marketing journey with you.

To Michael Davie of Manor House – many thanks for your faith in me, Michael, and for your dedication to fostering me as an author. This writing business is an interesting journey and I very much appreciate your insights and assistance.

To everyone else who has been involved with this book, or with my ever-growing understanding of the complexity of content marketing…and to my wonderful friends, family members and others who have been, and who continue to be, part of my adventure of life, thank You! The writing of a book might be a solitary occupation, but the environment out of which it comes is teeming with people and I am a lucky lady indeed to be surrounded by so many who care so much.

Susan Crossman, Oakville, Ontario

Introduction
Content Marketing / Social Media Context

I've been writing web content long enough to recognize the agony of uncertainty in a prospective client's voice when we start talking about their web presence. They know that they need to improve their online marketing efforts but they have no clue where to start.

And no wonder – the world of online marketing sometimes resembles a private club filled with experts who drop words like "algorithm" and "optimization" at the drop of a hat. They revel in their understanding of such topics as analytics and meta tags, and the assumption seems to be that if you don't know your inbound marketing funnel from your open rate then you've missed the boat. There might even be no hope for you.

Online marketing can be intimidating, no doubt about it, and I spend my days simplifying it for business people so they can generate more revenue as a result of their online activities. We focus on a subset of online marketing that currently flies under the label of "content marketing." By the end of this book I aim to help you figure out what that is, why it's important and how it works, and hopefully I'll be able to crack open a door to the future for you and your business that is filled with possibility.

The businesses my team and I help tend to have a few things in common:

- They know they need to improve their online marketing efforts but they just don't know how to get started.
- They suspect they might be losing out on customers that have actually been finding their competitors online instead of them.

- Some of them have attended an online marketing course or workshop and decided that content marketing was the "wave of the present." They became excited about the possibilities — but then went back to their businesses and the project went nowhere. (And, if that's you, I bet you're feeling pretty frustrated because you KNOW that this is important but you just haven't had the time, energy or knowledge to make it happen.)

- They might have started to develop an online marketing strategy at one point but it was a lot of work and it was confusing and they let the project slide in favour of easier, more important tasks.

- If they already have an online content marketing program they're now looking for new distinctions that will help them become more effective so they can increase their client base and grow their business.

- Or, finally, sometimes they've decided to improve their online marketing efforts and they know they need to do it, but their area of brilliance is not marketing and they realize they could really use some help and advice on how to make this happen.

Does any of that sound familiar?

Whatever **your** reasons are for exploring content marketing in more detail, please take heart. Although there are countless distinctions that can be made in this exciting field it is a process that can be taught, learned and duplicated. Once you have a program up and running, it's a straightforward way to generate more business as long as you're willing to cultivate your results with a fair bit of consistency. It takes time.

Constant change
We've all heard the old chestnut that reminds us that the only constant in our world is change itself, and I've found over the 30-plus years of my career that this is particularly true of

business and marketing writing. I'm old enough to have been writing when the internet first poked its opportunity onto my desktop computer and, in fact, I'm old enough to remember typing articles out on an electric typewriter. (Thank goodness those days are long behind us.) Resistance to the pace of change has proven futile in my career and had I decided to ignore the technological advances that merely heralded the arrival of the next ones, I would not have been able to maintain a career as a successful professional writer. So if I can give any advice to anyone who needs to get their message across to an important audience it is this: keep learning!

Furthermore, I believe that the revolution has only just begun and that we will continue to see an evolution in marketing and revenue generation as long as there is electricity (or whatever supersedes it) to power our mobile devices (or whatever supersedes them).

We are moving towards a world where a huge percentage of business is done online and if you are not playing in that field, eventually you aren't going to have a business. Pretending these changes aren't happening won't make them go away. And, while there still seems to be a place for direct mail in our marketing mix, and there is definitely a role for networking, I believe that developing and polishing our online content is the key to the kingdom.

Content marketing is an effective way to differentiate our businesses in the marketplace, while helping our perfect clients get to know, like and trust us. Most business people like to make money. Most of us would also like to make more money than we are currently generating. Let's face it, the effort required to build and run a successful business is huge. If we can find a way to streamline the process so that we can reach more people with less effort—and a moderate investment — wouldn't we want to do that?

Heck yeah!

My story:
I'm a career writer who started writing professionally decades ago, and, in fact, I have only ever worked with words. I've had stints as a journalist, a government communicator, a marketing copywriter and a corporate communicator. I'm also now the author of four traditionally published books. The first one, called "**Shades of Teale**," was a novel about a woman's experience of an abusive marriage. My second book, entitled, "**Passages to Epiphany**," was a collection of short stories and creative-non-fiction pieces about awakenings. My third the book, called "**The Write Way**," contained some of the writing wisdom I've collected up over the years that I think is imperative for other people – writers and non-writers alike — to know. And you are reading my fourth book here and now.

I have what I would describe as a magical life that allows me to balance career and motherhood, contribution and enjoyment. It's hectic. And it's working for me.

Seven years ago as of this writing, I was minding my own business, playing with my writing, working on my novel, spending every evening sitting on the porch chatting with my husband and planning both a trip to Barbados and the purchase of a lakeside cottage in Vermont. Life couldn't get much better. We lived in what appeared to be the biggest house in a beautiful suburban Canadian neighbourhood and we had worked hard to create the life we were enjoying.

So you can imagine what a shock it was when my 49-year-old husband was diagnosed with terminal stomach cancer. He was painfully ill for three months and then he died. Steve had been my high school sweetheart and we had two made young kids together who were, at that time, aged seven and nine years old. Our blended family also included my daughter from my first marriage and my two step-kids. It was a traumatic time for all of us and I was in shock at how quickly life can change. It was a miserable lesson. Not only had I lost my best friend, but I realized I had to kiss good-bye all my dreams of the future, get out of my 4,000 square foot house, and figure out how I was going to raise my kids, look after my mother, and plan for a mythical retirement Someday.

In the mirage of delight that came with being married to a man who at the time of his death had been a successful currency trader, I had not worked too hard in a few years. My business had become a pleasant hobby. It wasn't making anywhere near enough money to support my family. I dug in for a year or two of complete trauma and emotional chaos.

When the dust settled, I realized a lot had been happening in the business world while I had been more or less playing at being a writer. I was hearing strange words like "social media marketing" and "search engine optimization." This "content" word was being bandied about. And I realized I didn't have a clue how to run a writing business in an online world. So I rolled up my sleeves and learned everything I could possibly learn about how people were communicating and marketing themselves online. It was challenging, to be sure. And the process of learning about the intricacies of online learning convinced me of its power.

Content marketing is all about informing people without working too hard at selling them. The theory is that if you provide lots of valuable information you will show people that you are awfully good at what you do and lead them to a state where they know, like and trust you so much that they simply want to do business with you. The more ways you can find to do this, the bigger an online profile you can develop, and the more your business shines. If you do this well, you will make it obvious to anyone looking for the service you provide that you are the ONLY choice.
I don't believe that content marketing can replace personal networking for a service-based business. You still want face-

to-face opportunities to meet people and develop ways for them to get to know you and what you do. And there are many other strategies for marketing your business digitally. But your online content management strategy is a great way to support any other marketing you do. People might meet you at a networking event but if they are remotely interested in doing business with you they are going to search you out online.

So you want to have material available that routes people directly to you and you want the material people find online about you to be consistent with your brand.

Just for fun, I invite you to do an online search of you or your business. What do you find?

Next, search out a competitor.

Are there more references to them in the Search Engine Results Pages (SERPs)? Are those references posted on quality websites? Do they have a lot of links to their website?

Are your ideal customers more likely to find a reference to your competitor online than you? More and better content will help you shine online.

Your content drives your online rankings and the more organized and effective you are in developing your content, the more people know about you and the more you can grow your audience. You don't have to do it all at once, but you do need to get started. Is waiting until next month, next quarter, or next year — when you understand it better, or when you have "fewer other priorities"— going to benefit your business? There is no time like the present to get started.

So what can content marketing do for your business? Your online content marketing strategy gives you a bigger online footprint than you, as a small business, might otherwise generate. It should also:

- Allow people to find out more about you
- Help people see what working with you is like
- Show your target audiences who you are and what you can do
- Help educate people about how to improve their own businesses or lives
- Tell people that you are available as experts in your field and
- Increase your credibility

What's fun for me in working with my clients is watching their online garden grow – it takes time and effort but it's ultimately extremely satisfying.

The internet is a place of infinite variety and creativity and plenty of people are evolving new ways of using it in every moment of every day. Some catch on, and some don't. Some seem like a good idea for a while and then they don't.

But content is something that's been around for decades and so has marketing, and it's a good bet that telling a good story online is going to remain one of the most powerful ways to differentiate your business in a competitive market and give your potential customers good reason to do business with you.

This book is my effort to help you find your way through what can seem like a confusing world and I invite you to read it with the spirit of adventure that all explorers need when travelling through uncertain territory. There is nothing magic about content marketing. But the results can be magical.

Chapter 1

Content Marketing? What Does That Mean?

Back in the days before digital content marketing had ever been invented—in fact, before the internet had even been invented—I was a marketing copywriter for a marketing firm. I wrote brochures and sales letters, newsletter copy and advertorials. I laboured over the structure of my press releases and worked hard to bring zest to my bus ads. The marketing firm I worked for had a lot of clients and they all seemed to need a lot of marketing materials. The company was growing by leaps and bounds and I was grateful for the chance to make a living doing what I loved. It was a challenging job, however.

Sometimes the Writing Genie would favour me as soon as I sat down at my computer and other times I would stare cluelessly at my monitor wondering about a career change.
Where do all those words go when you need them in a hurry?

Deadlines screamed at me with frightening regularity and in the early days of my initiation into marketing, I concluded that a marketing firm can be a scary place for someone who likes a quiet environment, especially if The Boss has stress management issues. I survived, however, and somewhere around the time I left that firm to start a freelancing business, the Internet was invented and changed the game forever.

The point is, marketing is nothing new. Hundreds, if not thousands of years ago, people were looking for ways to market their products and services. They wanted to make a sale and, in order for that to happen, they needed a method of sharing the news about what they were offering, preferably in a way that had the people who needed what they were selling sit up and take notice. When I search the term "marketing" online today, a total of 1.86 trillion results show up; 295 million of them are definitions of what marketing is. That's a lot of definitions. In my own search for understanding, I've waded through ponderous, academic, scientific and homespun explanations that have actually failed to enlighten me about the nature of this massive beast. For a long time I thought there was something wrong with my own understanding, that I couldn't grasp something I was actually making a living at doing. What's more, every business person I meet knows that their company "needs some marketing." But what are they really asking for?

I took solace from the conclusion I came to and I invite you to take comfort in this wisdom as well: very few people actually know what marketing is.

What is Marketing?
So I've developed my own definition and it was as true in the days of the first radio broadcasts as it is in the age of digital communication: marketing is the process of starting conversations with the people who know they want what you are selling. The conversations themselves are what sales is about. So marketing starts the conversations that the salespeople handle.

You might start those conversations today at a networking event or a trade show. You might start those conversations by handing out brochures, business cards, newsletters or key chains. You might also start those conversations through your website, Twitter feed, Google + page or your blog. There are unlimited opportunities out there for starting conversations with people. But you want to make sure that you put your time, money and energy into starting your conversations primarily with people who might want what you are selling. And you want to make sure that the information you are giving them is the kind of information that might encourage them to talk to you.

And that's where your business might need help.

While you have been focused on handling the thousands of details that go into making your business successful, that one other issue, the one about marketing your company online, has been twisting in the wind somewhere beyond the back door of your place of business.

Somehow, while you were knee deep in refining your product line, developing your manufacturing processes, managing your sales staff, and doing whatever it takes to build your business to where it is today, you missed the memo that anxiously reminded you that you needed to develop an online marketing strategy that leverages the power of the internet to create more sales.

It's not too late.

There are many aspects to online marketing today and the field is in a continual state of evolution: what's current and effective today is going to change. As content marketing strategists, writers and project coordinators, me and my team help tell the stories that will start conversations that lead to sales for our clients. It's a process that lends itself to a lot of fine-tuning as we learn about the distinctions that will help our clients get more leads and generate more revenue. And it's really fun to watch a project take shape. The key task is to build a strategy around the unique aspects of the business's product, service and ideal customer base. And tell the company story with authenticity and enthusiasm across all channels.

There are other methods of online marketing that are effective as well, such as paid search and pay per click, website development projects that include conversion strategies and conversion architecture, and more. But without strong content that positions you as the top choice for the businesses and people you are here to serve, your other online marketing efforts are doomed.

What is Content Marketing?
Content marketing is about creating a substantial body of content related to your business and the needs of your ideal clients and sharing it through online platforms such as your website and your Linked In, Facebook, Twitter, You Tube and Google+ profiles. You want the content to tell your company story authentically so that it generates trust, credibility and likeability for you, and calls upon your viewers and visitors to take another step in a growing relationship with you.

Your online content is informational rather than blatantly "sales-y." And it has at its heart a respect for potential clients, acknowledging that they might want to some research before they engage in a conversation with a potential supplier. It builds trust and authority for you amongst your ideal customers and it supports your relationship with them. Providing helpful online content positions you as a valuable resource for people who need what you provide.

If you do this well, human visitors and search engines will reward your efforts and you will generate greater revenue as a result.

Did you know that some statistics estimate that 80% of all business transacted involves the internet in some fashion? And that up to 80% of business decision makers prefer to get company information in a series of articles rather than an advertisement? Many people report in surveys that content marketing makes them feel closer to the sponsoring company, and, that company content helps them to make better product decisions.

Doesn't it make sense that you'd better have a very strong presence online if you want to be competitive?

There are two ways to look at content: branded content that is strictly helpful, such as magazines about topics of interest in your industry or recipe booklets related to the product or equipment you manufacture; or content that relates to your business and the stories you can tell about it.

Red Bull Has This All Figured Out:

Red Bull is an energy drink company that runs something called the Red Bull Content Pool. It stocks more than 50,000 photos and 5,000 videos about sports, culture and lifestyle.

The company makes the material available to their 4.8 million subscribers, which tend to be TV stations, platform providers and cinema distributors.

Why?

Does the content they provide proclaim the benefits of drinking Red Bull, the beverage? NO! But it says reams about Red Bull as an adjunct to a lifestyle.

You can check this out for yourself at:
https://www.redbullcontentpool.com/content/international

Red Bull realizes that content marketing is all about informing and even entertaining people without working too hard at selling them.

The theory is that providing lots of valuable information will demonstrate to their target audience that they are experts in their field (in this case, an active lifestyle) and that they are so aligned with their target audience's needs and interests that they will, of course, resonate with the Red Bull product.

Red Bull is the drink for people who push the envelope of physical activity and so people will, of course, buy their beverages.

Red Bull is a large corporation with enormous amounts of money to throw at their content marketing strategy.

But you can get involved with content marketing, too, to the limit that your budget will allow. And the more ways you can find to do this, the bigger the profile you can develop, and the more you can stand out in a crowd of other people offering what you offer.

If you do this well, you will make it obvious to anyone looking for the product or service you provide that you are the ONLY choice in the field and your competition will fade into the background by comparison. And you will generate more revenue as a result.

That doesn't mean that it's time to give up on that quaint old-fashioned habit of meeting people face-to-face.

Your own unique process of making a sale still stands. It's just that your content marketing efforts will give your prospects more opportunities to get to know more about your company and what it can do for them. It supports your sales team and any other marketing you do.

People might meet you at a trade show or networking event, and like you on first impression. But as I mentioned earlier, if they are remotely interested in doing business with you, they are going to see what they can find out about you online.

So first of all, you want to HAVE material available that routes directly to your company, and, secondly, you want the material people find online about you to share positive and consistent messages about your business.

Action You Can Take Today:

Take an inventory of your web presence. Do you have:

A website that is less than three years old ☐

A blog that you update regularly ☐

A regular company newsletter ☐

A social media presence
(Twitter, Facebook, Linked In, Google+) ☐

Five+ professionally produced videos ☐

A press outreach program ☐

Five or more case studies on your website ☐

Five or more articles on your website
about your products or services ☐

A white paper that prospective customers
can download from your website ☐

A desire to improve your online presence ☐

Your Score:

10 checks = You've got this handled!
5-10 checks = You have some work to do
3-5 checks = Is it time to develop a strategy around this?

Less than 3 checks = It's still not too late to take action!

Chapter 2
Getting Started

There are a headache's worth of statistics out there about how well content marketing works. According to WebDam (http://www.webdam.com/2014-marketing-statistics-infographic/):

- B to B companies that blog will generate 67% more leads than companies that don't blog
- 52% of marketers have found a customer through Facebook
- 43% of all marketers have found a customer through LinkedIn
- Inbound marketing generates 54% more leads than outbound marketing

So, as you can see, the numbers support a strong content creation and marketing approach

Working Harder Versus Working Profitably:

The management of what you say about yourself and your business online is an intricate dance of story-telling and digital mastery: your online content affects both how you are perceived and how your business ranks in the search engines.

The goal is to use your stories to get results.

A lot of people I work with don't think they have any stories worth telling but when we get right down to it, almost everything they've chosen to do regarding the production, management and distribution of their product (or service) has at its very heart the stub of a story we could tell to encourage people to want to do business with them.

For example:

- A business that doesn't want to ask customers for testimonials because they are concerned about safeguarding customer privacy can create a blog post about how focused they are on their customers' confidentiality.
- A business that has been around for 30 years can create an interesting article about how their industry has changed over the past few decades (and how they have changed with it)
- Almost everybody can write case studies about projects they've completed
- Every case study can be turned into a power point presentation that can be posted to the web as a Slideshare presentation
- Slideshare presentations can be turned into videos
- Every time you post content to your website or other online platform you can tweet about it or create a status update sending people to the content (that you've posted to your website) so they can find out more
- And all of this content signals to the search engines that there is something good going on at your place of business, so they will reward you with better rankings

Story telling is an ancient art form and the people who study these things know that ancient humans crouched around campfires together sharing stories of strength and valour, passion and pain long before a printing press (or the internet) was ever a gleaming idea in a questing mind. A good storyteller has likely been a necessity in human society since the dawn of time and unlimited wisdom has been passed along painlessly through the vehicle of a good story.

Although the way we tell our stories has changed, their importance is just as significant today as it has always been: people are far more engaged by a good story well told than they are by a simple collection of facts packed together in an orderly row.

As most of us know, life (and business) is anything but consistently orderly and the lyrical surprises inherent in a good story catch our attention like nothing else can.

Which doesn't mean that the stories you want to tell about your business are epic romances or imaginative swashbucklers. Your online marketing stories need to be focused on helping your potential customers understand your product or service while lightening their load in some way.

So your content might include:

- Blogs (that tell a story)
- White papers (that include a story)
- Downloadable templates (that hint at a story)
- Free audio recordings (that include stories)
- Checklists to help them improve a process (not much story involved in a checklist)
- Facebook postings that point people to pertinent articles written by someone else (hopefully some stories in there)
- Linked In activity (business stories)
- You tube videos (video is all about the story)
- Slideshare presentations (that tell a story) and
- Podcasts (plenty of opportunities for telling stories here)

It's important that you post content consistently: A blog that is updated every six or eight months will add zero value to your online reputation whereas one that's refreshed weekly will pack a powerful punch. Your content needs to appeal to two separate audiences: the real people who might potentially buy from you and the web crawlers that want to know if you merit a Page One search ranking. So that means that your content needs to be cleverly written and cleverly optimized for search.

There is a lot to know about content marketing and it can seem confusing: As I mentioned earlier I started to learn about the field when the death of my husband required that the freelance writing "hobby business" I was pursuing needed to become a sustaining source of income for me and my two young children. I did not grow up in the digital age. I remember the breakthrough moment in my life when my parents gave me a cassette tape recorder as a birthday present. It completely eclipsed my poor little transistor radio.

I remember other "firsts" as well:
- The colour TV that moved in to the family room too late to add enjoyment to the hoop-la around the moon landing
- The eight-track tape machine that came with one of my father's company cars
- My mother's disapproval over the $80 handheld calculator my father simply had to have (Dad was an early adopter — that calculator could do nothing other than add, subtract, multiply and divide. My sister and I thought it was breath-taking.)
- The massive new microwave oven that took up residence on my sister's kitchen counter
- The home movie debates: VCR or betamax?
- And the wonder of the fax machine that majestically rolled out images from miles away in front of the wide-eyed crowd in my downtown Toronto office. How did they DO that?!

They were all miracles in their own way but nothing compared to the personal revolutions wrought by the internet. So my own learning curve on this issue was challenging and exciting. And, although content marketing is second nature to me now, I sympathize when my clients look with some bewilderment at the proposals I develop for them: when you aren't accustomed to how this all works, it can seem hugely overwhelming.

What Problems Do You Solve, And for Whom?

The key to any marketing is to be able to position yourself powerfully. That means matching your message to your market. That message needs to be so clear that people know immediately that you have what they want. Before any of that can happen, however, you need to know what problems you solve for people.

What pain are they in that you can eliminate? And what specific results can you deliver that will take them out of their pain? What relief do they yearn for in their businesses (or in their lives, if you are a B-to-C business) that you can help deliver? The answers to those questions are key, and you want to express the information in specific terms using simple language.

Different content marketers work differently and many web marketing companies purchase the content they sell to their clients through crowdsourcing sites where they can find plenty of inexperienced writers (whose first language is not always English) who are looking for work.

I was there once, too. But I don't think I ever had my prices down to $10 a page, as is common in today's market. The marketing companies then charge their clients $75 or so per page and pocket the difference.

What does $10 a page get you? Or even $75 a page. No offense intended to the people who are willing to write for peanuts, but let me ask you this. Is that $10 likely to include:

- Hours of 1:1 conversation with the business owner and/or his or her representatives so the writer can get a solid understanding of the business, the processes, the product or service being sold and the culture of the company?
- Hundreds of hours, over the course of a career, of writing training?
- Hundreds of hours of behavioural training?
- Years (perhaps decades) of solid marketing experience?
- Time spent labouring over finding the right words to convey the right messages?
- The time to care deeply about the outcome and the results?

Crafting a Conversation-Starter
These marketing companies might *think* that a $10 writer is just as good as a $300 writer for the purposes of representing a company online. After all, the search engines can't tell the difference. But what is *your* reputation worth? Every person who visits your website is going to form an opinion about you and your company based on what they read about you. Shouldn't that involve a sophisticated set of language skills that present you and your business in the best light possible? Doesn't your business deserve better?

And, really, if the idea of content marketing is to start the conversations that might lead to a sale, doesn't it make sense that those conversation-starters need to be well crafted?

I'm a little bit of over-kill in the writing department myself with training and experience few writers attain. I speak five languages (three well) and I have thousands of hours of training in writing, marketing, behavioural dynamics and how the brain works. The people on my team are similarly focused on continually learning more about our field. When we produce content for our clients, we bring a lot to the keyboard. We can't do all that for $10 a page.

When we develop a project for a business, we might find we need to:
- Do some work on the website
- Develop a blog
- Develop a newsletter
- Create content (case studies, articles, press materials, etc.)
- Establish an email marketing campaign
- Create a social media marketing and training campaign and/or
- Get their Google Analytics account set up or straightened out

Although we always start out with a finely crafted strategy to guide our efforts, there is a certain amount of "building the plane as we're flying it" as we learn more about an organization's customer base, its online infrastructure, and the unique challenges of communicating with customers. We are continually refining our efforts to get better results and customizing each client's program so it delivers what they seek.

We keep track of all the content we produce (and, by the way, we never post anything online that hasn't been approved by company representatives) and we pass the information about the content along to the sales staff so they can point their prospective customers to the work we've been doing.

Most small businesses prefer to start slowly with their content program and we are always open to discussing what that might look like. Alternatively, some of our clients stagger the introduction of the modules we propose so that every second month we might add something new, for example. Either way all elements of a content marketing program work together to create results together that are not possible with one element alone. The more you undertake, the bigger difference you can make to your lead generation results.

Need Some Great Resources to Find Out More?

Search the internet and you will find an enormous number of resources aimed at helping you with your content marketing initiatives. There truly are a lot of fabulous sites run by some very knowledgeable people who can provide you with more free information that will help you learn more about how to do all this yourself.

My own personal favourites include:

Hubspot: www.hubspot.com

Content Marketing Institute: www.contentmarketinginstitute.com

Copyblogger: www.copyblogger.com

Quick Sprout: http://www.quicksprout.com

It can be challenging to know exactly how to create the kind of content that will work best for your small business so here are some tips:

1. Be Clear about Who Your Audience Is:

Who is your ideal customer? Trust me, no matter how much you might want to believe that it's "Everybody," it isn't. The best marketing is highly targeted to a specific individual with specific problems and needs. You need to tailor your content around those needs so that it is clear to potential customers who you are, who you serve and how you help them.

2. Start with an Editorial Calendar:

It's important to be methodical with your content. An ad hoc approach to content creation and curation is not going to work. You need to be consistent and post regularly on topics that relate to your ideal customer. And you need to post content that covers the full range of products, services and issues you offer that are relevant to the people you serve.

3. Speak Plainly:

Don't default to "marketing speak" or the short-form lingo that works on either the shop floor or at your regular sales meetings. Your potential customers might not be familiar with terms that are second nature to you and your team. Do them (and yourself) a favour and say whatever you have to say in plain English.

4. Be original:

At least some of the information you will be including in your content could be applicable to your competitors as well. Make it easy for potential customers to spot your competitive advantages by highlighting the things that make your business stand out from the crowd. Sometimes this is also about the stories you have to tell about your company culture. Don't be afraid to tell your stories!

5. Post Content with Strong Visuals:

Including images and videos in your content adds excitement and increases visitor engagement. Text is a great way to tell your story but remember that a picture tells a thousand words and video brings emotion into the mix as well. They both help you tell a more powerful story.

6. Be Diverse:

As I mentioned, say "Yes!" to text, images and videos. But don't stop there. You also want to generate slideshows, eBooks, templates, and podcasts.

7. Don't Make Everything All about You:

Narcissism is never attractive and when you create content that harps upon your many wonderful qualities you are you are not demonstrating to your potential customers that you are good at listening and good at serving. Your prospects are looking for **evidence** that you will help them ease their pain and achieve their goals. Yes, make it clear why your product or service is a smart choice. But do it in a way that puts your potential customers first

8. Invite Engagement

Don't just create content, **invite** people to work with you! Tell them how to get their questions answered, show them how to obtain more information about your product or service, provide your contact information and, more than anything, give them the next step in the process of getting to know whether you are a good fit for what they are looking for. You don't need to knock them over with opportunities – but you do need to make it obvious how they can deepen the conversation if that is what they would like to do.

Don't be afraid to ask people to comment on your posts – you might not get a lot of feedback but at least let your visitors know that you value their input. And if you are lucky enough to generate a lot of commentary with your information, then you are taking important steps towards developing a community that will follow what you have to say and take an interest in future information that you might want to share.

9. Make It Interesting

You have eight seconds, *max,* to grab the attention of your website visitors and you aren't going to do that if your site is cluttered or dull. Use strong visual imagery and don't be afraid of colour. Headlines should be large and easy to read. And your text should be focused on your visitors and what they are looking for, Video has become an essential part of web content now and it's wise to invest in a professional videographer to help you tell your business story powerfully and professionally.

And What about a Content Marketing Strategy?

Ideally you want to wrap all of your content marketing initiatives into a logical strategy that summarizes and guides your content marketing program. The goals of a strategy are to:

1. Increase your company's online visibility

2. Communicate your company's unique strengths and attributes

3. Tell the stories that demonstrate your company's values and culture

4. Differentiate your company from others in its niche and

5. Increase lead generation.

The results available through content marketing tend to develop over time as newly developed content percolates through the web. The effect of each new piece of content builds upon the content created previously, both from a search engine and a human perspective. The point of creating a content marketing program is to generate more business and this is the guiding principle of all efforts Crossman Communications undertakes on behalf of our customers.

In fact, we rarely provide content marketing that is NOT part of a program – you really need to go about this in an organized fashion.

Ideally, a content marketing program should build on your existing reputation to make it easy for the decision makers among your prospective customers to:
  a) Easily find your company online

  b) Form positive opinions about your company based on what they see online, particularly in the areas of:

      - Customer Service

      - Creativity and

      - Product Performance

  c) Know and understand that your company has a sound business capability, an outstanding hands-on skill set and strong leadership

  d) Feel inspired by the example you set for other companies in its niche

A content marketing program is a tremendously creative endeavour and it's rewarding for companies to see their story unfold online.

We often find that new needs arise during the course of a content marketing program, and new opportunities present.

So, while the programs we recommend for businesses are based on our understanding of what our clients would like to achieve *today*, we are aware of the need to be flexible as we work together in order to provide the most value for the company.

Action You Can Take Today:

Where do you need to improve? Rate the following areas in terms of what you think needs the most improvement. Use a scale of 1 to 5 with 1 meaning "We've got this handled beautifully" and 5 meaning "We need to start here."

Your website   ____

Your blog   ____

Your company newsletter   ____

Your social media presence
(Twitter, Facebook, Linked In, Google+ etc.)   ____

Your videos   ____

Your press release program   ____

Case studies about the problems you solve   ____

Articles about your products or services
(and the problems they solve)   ____

Your white papers   ____

Chapter Three
Taking Another Step

Have you searched your company online lately to see what turns up? Try it just for fun and take a good look at the results.

Searching for your name, and your company name, will reveal all of the places on line where you and your company are mentioned… and it will give you a good sense of all the companies and other organizations that share a name that is either similar to, or exactly like, yours.

The people with whom you want to do business are not going to search for your company name if they don't know about you, so this isn't about how well you're showing up in a search. But taking an inventory of all the listings you have online will give you a sense of how robust your online presence actually is.

When I first did this exercise some years ago I was confronted with the shocking fact that I am not the only Susan Crossman in the world. I had already learned that there was a real estate agent in California with the same name as me, and she owned what I considered highly desirable: www.susancrossman.com.

But there are also other Susan Crossmans in various locations throughout the US and Canada, as well as the UK, South Africa, Australia, Spain and so on. If someone knew my name, but didn't know much else about me, how would they know they had the right Susan Crossman?

There was also another Crossman Communications in the world and it provided PR services in Australia. And it still does. Fifty years ago, another company that far away would not have any relevance at all to a business established in the Toronto area. But the internet now provides instant access to any business with a website anywhere in the world. Someone searching for your business could find the other guy instead, and not end up completing a sale that would benefit you both.

If I had known in the early days what I know now, I would have purchased www.susancrossman.com (if it were, indeed, available) when I set up my very first website. I do own www.susancrossman.ca and various other extensions (.net, .org, .tv, etc.) and the .com extension has subsequently become available.

But my company had always been called Crossman Communications and it initially didn't occur to me that I might also want the url that goes with my personal name as well. Those urls are cheap — generally speaking they cost only $10-$20 a year — and well worth the price. Likewise, I have also purchased numerous other extensions for Crossman Communications, in order to protect my brand. The world is shrinking!

I buy all of my urls through www.namecheap.com but there are many other services out there that will facilitate a url purchase such as:

www.godaddy.com
www.bluehost.com
www.domain.com

If you are interested, go to one of those websites and search for and purchase domain names that go with your company name, your own name, or how you do what you do. Buy misspellings of your name as well. If you're a Canadian company, purchase both the Canadian and American spellings if there is a word in your name that changes when you cross the border. It's a good idea to also purchase urls that go with what you do, or that people might use when searching for the type of service you provide, e.g. "safewheels.com" or "greattools.com," etc. You can easily point all traffic that finds you when someone searches for these words back to your website.

Online marketing of any sort strives to funnel traffic back to your website where visitors can engage more with your brand, get to know more about your business, and start conversations that might lead to a sale.

Your content is one of the most important tools available for helping that relationship develop.

Going back to that interesting idea of searching your company name online, you should find that your website is one of the places that shows up on the list of sites that the search engines find. And, if you have been doing a reasonable amount of content marketing, all of the places where you have been posting content should show up as well. If you haven't yet started populating the internet with content about your company, well, I guess now is as good a time to start as any!

Although people who haven't heard about you yet will not be searching for your company name, it's possible that you might meet someone at a trade show or networking event who will run a search for your business afterwards.

If you're telling your company story in a number of places online you will be helping those people develop a strong sense of what you do, how you do it, how you can help them, and why they should do business with you.

Different online platforms give you the opportunity to share different nuances about your business. For example, while all of your online profiles need to be completely professional in how they portray your business, you might decide to post a photo of the company picnic on Facebook... but probably not on Linked In.

Your blog might talk about some of the challenges you've faced in building your company to where it is today, and your You Tube videos might show how amazing your equipment is and how great your customers think you are. But every platform is another opportunity to tell another piece of your story in a way that invites visitors to take another step along the road to discovering how you can help them.

The people who don't already know about your business are not going to search for your company name and see what shows up. They are going to search for what they think they are looking for, and see what shows up. In other words, they are going to key into the search box the words that they feel relate to what they are looking for, and the search engines are going to spit out millions of entries that they think relates to those words.

Creating content that appeals to your customers is one thing – but there is a whole other level of understanding required in order to create content that appeals to the search engines. Your goal is to convince the search engines that when someone searches for what you offer, you are a perfect match.

The more active you are in creating and using profiles for your company on reputable sites, and the more content you produce for others to view, the more seriously the search engines are going to take your business when it comes to ranking how relevant what you offer is to your ideal customers.

In other words, your content is a key way to extend your online reach and signal to the search engines that
a) You are active online and
b) You are worth finding

So, to a large extent, your online content drives your online rankings and the more organized and effective you are in developing your content, the more people know about you, and the more you can grow your audience and get more online attention. There are a lot of other issues involved in online marketing as well but when it comes to content, more is always better.

You don't have to do it all at once. Your content creation efforts are a cumulative process and we all have to start somewhere, which is, quite often, with almost nothing! What's fun for me in working with my clients is watching their online garden grow – it takes time and effort but there's something very satisfying about watching a business's online footprint increase over time.

One of our clients had been sporadically posting occasional press releases to a "News" section on their site for several years and they hired us to improve their content marketing efforts. The Search Engine Results Pages (SERPs) gave a few listings under their company name and a search for their competitors showed a varying commitment to creating content. Within six months we had boosted their SERP placement and increased visits to their website substantially, through a consistent content creation and curation strategy that included the development of case studies, a monthly newsletter, a consistent press release strategy and a social media program.

It's not usually an accident that a company has a berth on Page One of the search rankings, especially if they are in a highly competitive field. It's a coveted position and it can take a great deal of dedication to get there and stay there.

If you aren't creating any content related to what you do and how you do it, you probably are not going to show up on the first or second page of search engine results when people search for the problems you solve or the product you sell. I've worked with some clients who didn't show up in the first 20 pages of search when we first started working together.

But if you have an active content marketing strategy that focuses on the issues and concerns of your audience, you will increase your online search position. Do it well and do it consistently, and you have a chance of getting to Number One.

As we saw earlier, "content" really relates to the content of your online real estate — all the words, images and videos you post to the internet that talk about the needs and problems of your ideal customers or clients. It positions you and your business as experts in your field. Your online "real estate holdings" are potentially unlimited but, unfortunately, most of us have limitations on the amount of time, money and energy we can spend looking after all that property.

So even though you *could* put details about your business up on hundreds of profile sites, you probably won't, at least in the beginning.

However much you can gracefully manage is the right amount.

According to the Content Marketing Institute (CMI), we're now living in a world where businesses need to become media companies in order to successfully compete for business. (http://contentmarketinginstitute.com/wp-content/uploads/2014/10/2015_B2B_Research.pdf). This is especially true when the economy is struggling. The CMI's research shows that 70% of companies surveyed are planning to spend more money on content marketing this year than they did last year, and they're using an average of 13 different online channels to tell their company story. Forty-two per cent of survey respondents post new content daily or multiple times a week.

More than half of the CMI's survey respondents find that their biggest challenge with content marketing revolves around producing enough engaging content.

Ultimately, it doesn't look as though content marketing is going anywhere, at least in the short term, although I can pretty much guarantee that it is going to continue to evolve. If you haven't jumped into this particular pool yet (or even if you have), it might be helpful to take my "Content Marketing QuickStart" survey and ask yourself:

1. What are your objectives for your content marketing strategy? (e.g. do you want to generate more revenue, increase engagement with potential customers, influence opinion, share your philosophy, support your brand, position your company representatives as thought leaders in your industry, etc.)

2. How are you going to measure success? (e.g. increase visits to your website, grow your database, increase downloads of an eBook on a particular topic, increase sales of a particular product or service, increase followers on your Linked In page, etc.)

3. Who is your ideal customer? (there's that question again: what business are they in, what position do they hold in that company, how old are they, where do they live or work, what education or training have they acquired, what pain are they in around the work they do, etc.)

4. What problems does your business solve for them? (e.g. do you save them time, energy or money, clarify problem areas in their work, decrease stress in their world somehow, etc.)

5. What content could you provide for them that would provide value and show you are focused on helping them? (e.g. a white paper that explains changes in an industry or process, a video that demonstrates how to do something more effectively, a webinar that reviews a process or procedure, a blog series that explains changes in an industry or piece of legislation, etc.)

I find that when people start looking at their content as a powerful tool, rather than a mysterious expense, they start to realize how valuable it is. A content marketing strategy will answer all of the questions above, plus set out a schedule for adding to your existing content holdings at regular intervals. For example, my clients usually have a schedule where we write one blog post or one article weekly, we produce one Slideshare presentation a month, we post to our social media sites daily and we review our Google Analytics regularly so we know which pieces of content are generating the most interest. That allows us to fine tune our content to match visitor interest.

My very first foray into content production, aside from my first website, of course, was my blog. I went to a social media marketing workshop and at the end of three hours had managed to set up my Twitter, Linked In and Wordpress blog accounts. I got very excited about this idea of writing a blog.

I'm a writer – a blog should be easy for me. And it more or less was.

I hadn't been told how to develop an editorial schedule or to really target the needs of my clients and potential clients but I jumped in and started writing about whatever struck my fancy. Lo and behold, nothing happened.

For six months.

I'd been told to stick with it and remember that a blog was not a fast path to cash (it generally isn't) but I think I could have generated more results faster if I'd been more strategic in the beginning with what I was saying and who I was targeting. I had put no thought to my messaging, I had no editorial schedule and I had no calls to action. As I went along and learned that these were all important parts of the content creation continuum, I began to get more and better results.

I also didn't have a clue what Google Analytics was, or how it might help me boost my efforts.

Success with content comes from three factors:

    a. Staying True to Your Brand

    b. Posting Consistently

    c. Paying attention to your Google Analytics results

In the beginning, I was all over the map and my results reflected my lack of focus. I didn't really know what I was doing. And I wasn't clear about my brand. But fast forward a number of years and my blog is an important part of lead generation for my business and I do my level best to produce a new blog each and every week.

As my business has developed, my blogging strategy has needed to keep pace…and, truth to tell, it hasn't. Some of the services Crossman Communications offers have morphed into a whole new, separate business and I realized about a year ago that I actually run two businesses: a content marketing business and a book coaching and editing business. This hasn't been reflected in my web presence and I've been slowly doing the things I need to do to change that.

This has a lot to do with branding and we'll talk more about that in the next chapter.

Action You Can Take Today:

Search for your business name online and list all the places where your business has a listing or a mention.

Search for your industry and/or the product or services you provide, and list the top five.

Search for the top five results from your industry/product search, and find out what their "online real estate portfolio" looks like.

List five actions you can take to start extending your own online presence.
Do one of them right now.

If you feel you need assistance with any of the above, please reach out to Crossman Communications at susan@crossmancommunications.com.

Chapter Four
We Have to Talk about Your Brand

The elephant in almost every board room I enter is the issue of my client's brand.

Their brand triggers an enormous range of emotions, from frustration, to boredom, to annoyance and, yes, even anger. Like marketing in general, branding seems to be one of those things that people just don't "get." Or want to.

Many business people think branding is a code word for their logo.

Well, yes, and it's so much more than that. It's about what that logo represents.

Let's take a deeper look.

Content marketing, being a type of marketing, strays into the topic of branding and if you are one of those people who would rather watch paint dry than talk about branding, please bear with me. This will help you generate more revenue. And it is so much more efficient than ignoring your brand and hoping for the best.

When it's done properly, a branding research project is conducted over a number of months and results in a massive document that is full of key information about your company, your ideal customers, your competitors and your opportunities.

It can cost many thousands of dollars. And it will create suggestions for getting the most out of your marketing communication dollars (the ones you *haven't* spent yet).

A branding exercise will stray into the ever-important area of your logo, as well as the key true messages your ideal customers need to hear about you in order to know that you are the ideal supplier for them. It conveys emotion and personality. Your branding has an awful lot to do with your ideal customer. And, in an ideal world, your content follows your branding.

A lot of branding experts will tell you that your brand represents the promise you make to your customer about what they can expect from your products and services. It differentiates your business from those of your competitors, and it expresses who you are, who you want to be and who people perceive you to be.

Are you the innovator in your industry? The creative problem-solver? The high-cost, high-quality option, or the low-cost, get-the-job-done alternative?

You can't be all things to all people and who your brand paints you to be should be founded upon who you really are and who your target customers want and need you to be. Ideally, these match perfectly.

The foundation of your brand is your logo. Your website, packaging and promotional materials – all of which should integrate your logo – communicate your brand.

If you haven't investigated your brand yet, and you haven't formalized the information you've accumulated about it in a document that anyone can read, the people who create content for you are going to have to guess about what your target customers need to know about you in order to find you appealing.

Some of us marketing writers are darned good guessers. But we don't have all the answers to everything.

Once you have developed the database that equals your brand statement, you can hand it to your writers and graphic designers and they can embed it into all the content they create on your behalf. It will function as a guide to creating your website and absolutely everything else you write, or anyone writes for you.

Where there is no branding document to guide a company's marketing efforts, this is what often happens:

I'll ask my client, who is generally either the CEO or President, but often the General Manager of the company: "Who is your ideal client?"

And they'll say: "Everybody."

Well, it's hard for me to write to appeal to an "everybody."

But I CAN write to appeal to a 40-year-old male maintenance manager who is on his feet all day, hears regularly from his boss about how the safety record at the company is its number one priority, needs to continually do more with less and would rather not try a new supplier if it means burning bridges with the old one. The devil we know…

As a small business where every dollar counts, you can't afford to talk to everyone. You have to start conversations that might lead to a sale with the people who are likely to buy what you're selling. "Everybody" doesn't need what you offer.

But your ideal customer is eagerly scanning the horizon of their world hoping you will show up in it someday. THOSE are the people your marketing should be targeting so you can maximize your chances of find them.

So roll up your sleeves for a minute and let me help you unravel this one. My company does not provide branding consulting services at this point but over the years we've worked with three different branding companies and me and my team are continually on the lookout for new distinctions in this area. And we've barely scratched the surface about what there is to know about branding.

The branding for my own company is not something I'm waving the flag about as of this writing – my business has changed since our last re-brand, our website needs upgrading, our marketing materials need to be refreshed and another re-brand is on the radar for the next year or two. Will we ever catch up? Goodness me, I hope so.

Sound familiar?

I'd like to point out that we are growing anyway. But we would do it so much more elegantly, and quickly, I'm sure, if we had the resources to devote to a complete re-brand, especially now that the company has evolved past its original form. It is on my vision list for the company. And bear in mind that our writers know our business, and our clients, quite well. We still need branding services.

What Goes into Getting Clear on Your Brand?

It does take some time and effort to do this work and that might be why a lot of businesses leave it off their "wish list."

Whether you plan to coordinate it all internally, or hire someone else to do the leg work for you, it's probably helpful to get guidance from someone who specializes in branding, since they know the questions to ask and they are quite often experts in graphic design, which is a key element of your brand expression.

The assistance will be helpful because your brand requires you to get clear on:

- Your ideal customer
- Your company's values
- Your company's "personality"
- Your vision for your company
- The issues that differentiate your company from your competition
- The main benefits of your products or services
- The ways you are better than other companies
- The advantages of other companies' products or services
- The things other companies are doing that you could do be doing too –with your own "twist"
- The areas of excellence that you don't talk about
- Your customer's values

- The products or services that you want to grow
- The products or services that you should consider dropping
- The products or services your customers love
- The products or services your customers don't care about
- The aspects of your business that your customers love

- The aspects of your business that your customers wish you would improve

- What you could do to improve your marketing

- The visual imagery that is likely to appeal to your ideal customers

- A lot more other stuff as well

That's a lot of information to accumulate, analyse and summarize and it's easy to get lost in detail.

The point of acquiring all that information is so that you can package it up into marketing materials — your logo, your website, your brochures, your online content and anything you're your company produces to speak for it — that will immediately appeal to your ideal customers.

So who is Your Ideal Customer?

The more you know about who you want buying your product or service, the more effective you can be in launching an appeal to them.

You probably have a lot of information about these people already, or at least your salespeople probably do.

You just might not have summarized it in a way that someone else, such as a content marketing expert, can use to create content that is appealing. Let's go a little deeper with this one:

What You Need to Know About Your Target Audience

Some branding experts want to know details about your ideal customer that might even include the kind of toothpaste they use (yes, there are times when that could be important).

But, generally speaking, here is what will be helpful to know:

1. Demographics
The people who are creating content (or logos or websites) on your behalf need to know as much as possible about your target audience, specifically their:
- Age
- Gender
- Education
- Occupation
- Income Level
- Status: married, single, children, retired

2. Geographic and Lifestyle Factors
How do the people you are trying to attract live – and where?
- Are they rural and have to drive everywhere?
- Or do they live in cities and take transit to work?
- What kind of weather is typical for the area?
- Are they spenders, or are they conservative with their money?

3. Customer Needs
What does your ideal customer need? What pain are they in, and why? For example, is just-in-time delivery important to them? Or has safe storage of supplies been an issue lately? Are they under increasing pressure to "green up" their processes?

4. Behaviours
When you look at your customers' behaviour over the past few years can you see any trends? Will they sacrifice quality for price in some areas but not others?

5. Psychographic Details
Are there any personal traits typical to your ideal customer? Are they early risers? Fans of one sport over another? Do they favour Android, Blackberry or iPhone? Do they get their news on TV or via the internet?

Once you've found answers to all of this information you can start to put together a detailed profile of your ideal customer. In marketing-speak, we call this a "Persona."

You may have different personas for the various products or services that your business offers.

Give them each a name, a code word that represents all of the people who might possibly want what you are selling.

To show you what that just might look like, I'll let you take a peek at the persona that we've developed for the Crossman Communications ideal client.

I would now like to introduce you to Jim, a.k.a My Ideal Content Marketing Client:

Demographics:
- He is a 57-year-old married man living in a large North American city
- He earns a comfortable living from a successful manufacturing business that he has either built from scratch or taken over from his father
- He has two children who are finished with their education and who have left home
- He is university educated, with a degree in Life
- Since graduating from university, he has never seriously worked anywhere other than in the business he has been building for the past 20+ years
- He has an international outlook and business vision

Day-to-Day
- A typical day starts around 6:00 am with a cup of good coffee, a run-down of the headlines and a review of any emails that have come in overnight
- Home is a comfortable residence in a nice neighbourhood that Jim shares with his wife, Laura (who works part-time as a nurse) and an aging dog, Hank, who has been with the family for many years
- He has two vehicles – a Ford pickup truck that is useful around the plant and a Cadillac CTS that is an absolute delight to drive on weekends

- Jim and Laura take two good holidays every year – in the early spring and in late fall

- Fun is about getting together with friends for a barbecue or poker night, seeing the kids when they come home, meals out, watching hockey

- Jim is intense about his work but he has a good sense of humour. He is not particularly interested in spiritual conversations and will go to church on occasion, although Sundays tend to be a day for sleeping in a little and getting some rest if possible; he likes spending some time by the pool catching up on the news

Pain

- Jim has worked hard his whole life to build his company to where it is today. It's been tough but he has created a good measure of success. Now he wants to break through to a new level of revenue. He wants to double earnings and he isn't sure how to go about it. He knows it involves marketing, an area he hasn't invested a lot of time and energy into developing. His team is great at sales, though.

- His pain, therefore, is that he needs to get some marketing but he doesn't understand how this brave new world of online marketing works – it seems very confusing

- He doesn't know how to go about hiring someone to do the marketing for him, or how to determine if the person offering marketing services is going to do a good job

- He knows he has to start soon – in fact this should have been on the radar a year or more ago — but he's so busy he is feeling overwhelmed right now

- He wants some help – but who should he trust?

Goals
- Set up a content marketing program that will tell his company's story to the people who need what he's selling
- Improve his company's search engine rankings
- Reach a wider audience
- Generate more revenue

Other
- Jim's company website was set up by a friend's cousin three or four years ago.
- He has a profile on Linked In. For some reason.
- He thinks Twitter and Facebook are silly
- His business has some videos up on YouTube that they shot in order to show the equipment and the plant

Because I know Jim, more or less personally, I think about him every time I write something for my business.

I have also given Jim's information to the graphic designer who creates visual content for my business (including the new website I'm investing in), and anyone else who might create marketing materials for us.

I don't have to have a long drawn-out conversation with anyone I hire to service my business – I just hand them Jim's persona details and they know immediately who I would like to have conversations with about the services my business provides. It is so simple – and I *like* simple.

Your persona is an important part of developing your brand but it's not the only piece.

Ideally you also need to delve into your competitive advantages, your services, your brand and your competition.

But when you get right down to it, your marketing isn't about you. It's about your ideal customer.

Once you have established a persona, you can start exploring the words and images that are going to resonate with them. You do that by familiarizing yourself with your ideal customer's biggest problems — and the solutions you offer.

Action You Can Take Today:

Build the persona that represents your ideal customers. (You can ask Jim for help.)

Include information that includes that person's:

- Demographics

- Geographic and Lifestyle Factors

- Their needs and the pain they are in that you are uniquely suited to solving

- Purchasing or other Behaviours

- Psychographic Details

Chapter Five
Writing for the Web

I meet a lot of people in the course of an average week and I always divulge my occupation with a mixture of sweet pride and delight. I consider writing important work, and whether I am creating web content for one client or editing a book manuscript (another service Crossman Communications offers) for another, I get to feel the satisfaction that comes from being of service. And it's such a fun job!

Not everyone has taken that path. I'm all too aware that English grammar is not drilled into the heads of young people now the way it was when I was a scrawny 10-year-old pondering the difference between an indirect object and a subject completion. There are an awful lot of rules in English grammar and it's not everybody's bag of chips.

But I'm convinced that language facility in general, and English grammar in particular, can contribute much to success in life. It's especially important in an online world where people make judgments in nano seconds and can bounce off a website faster than a goldfish can forget your name.

Express yourself well and convincingly, however, and you open the doors to all manner of important life transactions: more customers for your business, better relationships with friends and colleagues, support for a cause you value, promotion to that job you wanted...whatever you want is yours if you can win the attention and support of other people. The tool we all use to do that is language. So of course, the more skillfully we can use that tool, the greater our results will be on all fronts.

And while I believe that literacy is a major key to financial success on an individual basis, Statistics Canada has been busy pointing out that a population's literacy skills have a bearing on how well that country performs economically as well.

Canada's labour market — and that of many other developed countries — has evolved from being based primarily on manufacturing and agriculture to one that emphasizes services.

This change has engendered rising skill requirements and there is a concern as to whether or not literacy skills in this country have improved apace.

If you are an American reading this book, please don't feel too smug – the statistics are even worse for the USA. We operate in a globalized information economy now, as the internet all too nicely highlights: Can we meet that challenge?

According to the Conference Board of Canada, the literacy skills of 40 per cent of Canadian adults are too low to be fully competent in most jobs in our modern economy (Source: http://www.conferenceboard.ca/hcp/details/education/adult-literacy-rate-low-skills.aspx).

The International Adult Literacy Survey from which this information was derived, determined that in the United States that figure was an even more disturbing 48 per cent: (http://www.oecd.org/edu/innovation-education/adultliteracy.htm), (some sources claim that it has risen to 53 per cent in the years since that study was completed). This is not good news for us, people! (http://www.conferenceboard.ca/hcp/details/education/adult-literacy-rate-low-skills.aspx).

The Conference Board further notes that one-quarter of all adults in the Canadian labour force are only marginally literate, which obviously has serious repercussions on their ability to understand and follow written directions. Improving the literacy skills of this group would deliver significant positive results for employers, in terms of productivity, innovation and bottom line results.

The employees themselves would benefit from higher earnings, better work performance and better quality of life overall.

The ability to communicate clearly is obviously an advantage for businesses. And individuals. There are reams of information available online about writing and there are many excellent books that walk the same path. (My book, ***The Write Way***, provides some assistance with the task of writing well and it's available on amazon.com:

http://www.amazon.ca/The-Write-Way-Becoming-Successful/dp/189745340X).

Every writer brings a dash of their own personality into their insights and so you are probably finding that this book reflects the approach I tend to take in the work I do.

What Does That Have to Do with Online Marketing?

The short answer is that, in my opinion, good writing is important for almost anything you want to do, including tell your story well online.

And I wave the banner for quality in this area, unpopular though that is in a world where you can crowdsource a page of content for $10. An awful lot of digital marketing experts think it's foolish to spend more money than you absolutely have to on something as perceptively low-value as writing? Argh!

I have a story that might be relevant here that relates to how I learned to write for the web. And I actually, I started to learn how to write for the web by learning how to write for an audience. It's still about marketing, ladies and gentlemen. Here's how the story went:

The Magic of Marketing Copywriting:

The head of the marketing agency I wanted to work for leaned back in his chair and lit another cigarette. He squinted at me through the choking haze of smoke swirling around his head and he gave me a keen, appraising look. This was his company, his office and his building, and the anti-smoking police had not been notified of his continuous flouting of the law against smoking in the workplace. I think now that most of his non-smoking employees had been too scared of the man to dare whimper a word of objection.

I had set up this interrogation weeks earlier when the agency's Vice-President told me I had passed the first round of interviews for a copywriter's position and it was up to The Boss to either green light or deep-six my application. We were only three minutes into the interview and already it wasn't looking good.

The Boss finally leaned forward in his chair and, still squinting, said nothing. I was reminded of Clint Eastwood in one of those cheesy old Western movies. Clint would squint mercilessly at the landscape, too, and then head out to gun down a whole town full of nasty characters. Although I was wearing, as I recall, a cream coloured suit with a pretty turquoise blouse, I wondered, for a moment, if I actually looked like someone of evil intent. This interview was not getting any better.

A massive cup of coffee balanced precariously on a tall and very messy stack of papers on the edge of The Boss's desk, and a jumbled bookshelf off to the left invited my attention. A gumball machine stood on a stand in one corner of the office and a heavy stressed leather jacket had been flung, artistically, almost, over the chair beside me. And still he said nothing.

I sat and looked around the room, pretending that this kind of silence between two strangers was a perfectly normal part of my professional career. I wondered what on Earth this guy was thinking. It was the verbal equivalent of waiting for someone to blink and I was determined not to be bullied into blinking. The Boss needed a copywriter. I was, at the very least, a writer, and I had experienced quite a lot of success in my field, up until that very brittle moment in time. Fresh from a year off as a new mother, I was looking for a job that did not require a lengthy commute and I figured, in the cocky way of the very young, that I could do anything. Even write marketing copy. Even without any experience. Even without any training.

How hard could it be?

I leaned back comfortably in my own chair and crossed my ankles, as I had been taught to do as a young girl. I casually leaned down and tugged my portfolio out of the battered briefcase I had dug out of the bottom of a closet, and I set the accordion file containing my clips on the only corner of the desk that had not been attacked by the kind of creeping clutter that begs for professional attention. I waited. He waited.

Finally, after what seemed like enough time to finish seven innings of an average baseball game, the great man spoke.

"So?" he said.

"So?" I repeated. It would have been nice if he could smile, and I thought he might have quite a nice face if he ever deigned to wrestle it into a cheerful expression. As it was, he looked dour and critical. He had a beard and a mustache, hair down to his shirt collar and gray-blue eyes that were framed by exceedingly long eyelashes. He was tall and lanky. Graceful. Possibly sleep deprived. What on Earth did this man want?

"So you say you're a writer." It was a question. Not a very nice one.

"I *am* a writer," I said archly. He instructed me to pull out my best clips and I did. Feature articles from the London Free Press, a daily newspaper. Feature articles from Canadian Press, the nation's newswire service. Press releases, speeches and media backgrounders from the Ontario Ministry of Health, THE largest provincial ministry. In. All. Of. Canada. One after another I pulled them out of my file and pushed them across the desk for his review.

After approximately 184 seconds he looked at me and snarled.

"What is this crap?" he asked. My heart sank. It was the best I could do, in point of fact, and plenty of people had told me it was great stuff.

My introduction to marketing was less than stellar. But I got the job anyway. What followed was three years of metaphorical head-banging and actual hand-wringing, loud arguments and quiet consolations, discussions, explanations, frustrations and breakthroughs as I teased out of my reluctant mentor the strategies and techniques that were to turn me into a solid marketing copywriter. He patently did not want to teach me. But I was the best he had found and, dad gummit, he was going to work with me.

The problem, dear readers, is that writing marketing copy is nothing like writing news articles or press releases or briefing notes. Those communication vehicles require, more or less, little more than the solid recitation of factual information.

They require great research and interview skills, a nice way with people, a solid sense of how to organize information and a terrific command of the written language. A little wide-eyed guile doesn't hurt. And a plan is essential. It's not that it's easy to do all of the above. It's just that it's much easier than writing hard core marketing copy.

There were many times during my marketing apprenticeship all those years ago when I felt my heart tackled by terror and my legs gripped by a strong urge to run. Was I ever going to figure this out? On many panicked mornings, as I drove to the office, it seemed unlikely. And I did. Finally.

It would have helped to have had a little context from which to work and so I'll repeat, yet again, my favourite definition of marketing. Actually, it's my own definition, and one I developed after the umpteenth person asked me, "So, what is marketing, anyway? You've read the words here before: marketing encompasses all of the activities you need to do in order to start conversations with people who are likely to buy from you. Like create a website, a Linked In profile, a You Tube video or a direct mail piece. Or maybe launch email marketing or pay per click campaign, deliver a speech, write a blog, send out a newsletter, write a book, give talks. The possibilities are endless and most of them require you to write something.

Writing strong marketing copy requires you to give up any illusion you have ever had about what is important in the world. Because most of us assume that what's important to us is important to other people as well. We think that we need to send our potential customers avalanches of information that tell them how amazing we are.
Gong!

When you're writing your web content, or any marketing material, really, you rarely want to write about how great you are. Because your perfect client doesn't really want to hear about you. Your perfect client wants to hear words that demonstrate how well you understand the agony he or she is going through in getting through just one more day of their lives without the assistance you can provide.

They want to know that you understand, down to the smallest detail, how much they are suffering. They want a ray of hope in a bleak world.

They want to know that you understand their pain.

But first of all you have to know who "they" are.

Rule number one in writing your web and other marketing content is to figure out who is going to buy what you're selling. (We've talked about this before. It's still important!)

The answer is not "everybody." Nor is it "anybody." Out there, somewhere, is a demographic of individuals who are the perfect recipients of what you have to offer. And the more narrowly you can define them, as we noted in our last chapter, the easier it is to get them to flock to your product or service. Trust me on this one.

Which, again, is where the pain part comes in.
What keeps them up at night? How are they suffering? What do they want more of or less of? What makes them crazy and what makes their heart sing? You want to crawl inside the skin of your perfect customer and wear their lives so you know, really *know*, down at the drooling, bended knee pit of their worst day, how you can help them get back on the fast track, where they really belong.

And what *can* you do to help?
While you're lying on your belly on the floor beside your perfect customer, and they are stifling moans of frustration as

they manfully pretend there is nothing wrong, you want to gently, very gently, paint for them a picture of how you can help their miserable wind-sucking problem disappear into thin air so you can transform their world into a complete masterpiece of comfort and delight.

Of course you are never, Ever going to lie to anyone in your web copy. Always Tell the Truth. Which requires a little work on your part because you need to figure out what the Truth actually is, and that's why you need to go through an in-depth branding exercise before you even consider writing your own web copy.

What is your Truth?

For Pity's Sake, Brand Yourself!
I know I'm repeating myself. You need to find out what it is you do that no one else can do and you need to know who you do it for. This usually involves a branding process.

As I've said before, this is a microbial course of discovery in action that many entrepreneurs and business people sidestep because it is so much bloody darned work. It requires a level of self-analysis that borders on therapy. It is time-consuming and, if you do it with the assistance of a branding expert, it does cost money. Often an outrageous amount of money.

And it is worth every dime. Knowing the ins and outs of your brand delivers a wealth of information that is exceedingly useful in developing your web or other marketing copy. What do you offer and why is it better? Who do you serve and how do you serve them? What are your competitive advantages? What are you less adept at delivering? What promises do you and your brand make to your customers and clients? How much do you charge? And so much more!

If you're hiring a copywriter or a graphic designer, you can hand all of that written, codified branding information over to him or her and avoid the need for in-depth interviews or time-consuming telephone conversations that might start with the lurching, painstaking question, "So...what exactly do you *do?*" Your branding documentation explains the whole schmeer in minute detail and gives your earnest subcontractors a passel of priceless information that can help them present you precisely the way you need to be portrayed.

As a copywriter with years of experience and a mountain of exclusive training behind me, I can make highly educated and extremely intelligent guesses about what your brand might be.

I'm right a great percentage of the time. But do you really want to leave the definition of your business over to someone who is not you? What if you chance to hire a writer who *doesn't* have the scars, bruises and haggard appearance that summarize a life of learning marketing the hard way? What if they are full of confidence and bravado, and sit before you with clean fingernails and a collection of really great bohemian scarves... only to tell you they think it would be a great idea to highlight your previous job experience on the Home page of your website?

There might be times when that's a great idea. But generally, *NO*! Don't do it!

Talk about your perfect client's biggest challenges. And mention how you can make their life better.

Technicalities
There's a lot of technical information about online marketing available on the web that is about as captivating to read as a university text book. And some very smart people get paid enormous amounts of money to research, analyze and quantify

marketing information for those very same textbooks. There is a place for that.

But most small business owners are light on their feet and low to the ground. They don't have a lot of time to spend on anything other than revenue generating activities. They want the straight goods and they want to know where to spend their time and money so they get the biggest bang for the buck.

So what are the straight goods of online marketing copywriting? Aside from the points we've covered above (and elsewhere in this book), here's what I've learned:

1. **Use great headlines.** They keep people reading.
    - Numbers work well (e.g. "The Five Expert Secrets of Writing to Sell")
    - Action words are good, too (e.g. "Supercharge Your Sales!")
    - Words that speak to results are effective (e.g. "Double Your Revenue in Three Months or Less")
    - And ask questions (e.g. "Are These Writing Mistakes Costing You Money?")
    - There is currently some debate as to whether it's a good idea to use your keywords in headlines and I fall into the camp that stands in the middle of the internet playground wondering, "Well, why *wouldn't* I use keywords in a headline, if I can do it with finesse?"

2. **Keep it short.** Especially on the web. Statistics say you have anywhere from three to nine seconds to grab and hold a reader's attention so don't waste a single one. Use short, simple words, rather than fancy ones, vary the length of your sentences and include numbered lists or bullet points for maximum impact.

You aren't out to impress people with your vocabulary here. You are attempting to start conversations with the people who might want to buy what you are selling.

3. **Put your most important information up front**. Most readers are not going to stick around to the end of your web page, although some do. They scan. Don't you? If you're offering special pricing on an item for this week only, tell your readers sooner, rather than later, and make sure you stress *why* your product or service is important to your readers.

4. **Stress the benefits of what you offer.** It's nice that you're selling a pen that doesn't leak but what's going to matter to me, the reader, is what's in it for me. I'm a lazy thinker sometimes, so connect the dots for me. Sure, tell me the pen doesn't leak but also point out that, as a result, I never again need to deal with inky and potentially embarrassing messes in my laptop bag or jeans pocket.

5. **Use Active Voice.** Rather than tell me that "equipment you are replacing can be returned for secure disposal by us," say "we'll securely dispose of the equipment you are replacing." When you were in grade school, you might have seen that one expressed as "The dog was walked by the boy." It would be turned into "The boy walked the dog." Active voice represents a much more efficient use of words than passive voice, and it gets the point across much faster and with greater impact.

6. **Use positive words instead of negative ones.** "We want you to enjoy the benefits of lower payments" glides into the hearts of your readers so much more

easily than "We don't want you to struggle with high payments."

7. **Be assertive**. And stand up for how great you are. A statement like "We try to do our best on every project we undertake" does not fill me with confidence. But if you say "We aim to outperform the competition on every project we undertake," you'll get my attention!

8. **Be specific.** It's great to hear that your product or service helped many consumers or businesspeople succeed last year. But I'll be more convinced if you tell me how many people you affected, and how your efforts increased their success. Did their revenues or savings increase by an average of 29%? Did you help them increase their customer base by an average of 18%? Did they notice a drop in complaints from customers of at least 27% because of what you did? Give me the details!

9. **Engage the senses!** Embed words in your copy that give audio, visual and kinesthetic depth to your language. Is your product colourful, shiny, glossy or beautiful? Can people hear the words of praise their partners will be heaping on them when they tell them they engaged your services? Will they feel an intense pride of ownership or a heady thrill of achievement because of something you've sold to them? What emotional vibrancy can you include in your copy? Sense-oriented words rock the world of your reader – engage them!

10. **Avoid jargon**. Your field may be rife with pet terms that people "in-the-know" fling at each other with confident abandon. But your ideal customer might not know what those terms are, and there's a good chance they will tune out if they hear them and feel confused.

11. **Go easy on the adjectives.** I love an adjective as much as the next writer but I have to tone it down when I'm writing marketing copy. *And* when I'm writing fiction, oddly enough. Come to think of it, it's a good idea to use adjectives sparingly in almost all the writing you do, fun as they are. Adjectives — words that describes things — detract from the masterful train of effectiveness that you're trying to create with your language. But if you want to add some rocket fuel to your writing style, latch onto a horde of powerful verbs (action words) and see what happens.

12. **Tell a story.** Everybody loves a story. It doesn't have to be a long one and it doesn't have to be on your home page. If there is something unique about how you came to be in business, and if it ties in with your commitment to quality products and services, tell your readers about that. It helps position you as a real human being and will capture our imagination in a way that facts and figures will not.

13. **Use metaphors.** Dr. Gerald Zaltman and Dr. Lindsay Zaltman of Harvard University did extensive marketing research a few years ago and determined that seven metaphors consistently increase buying behaviour in people living in pretty well every country in the world. Check them out and use them! (http://www.marketingmetaphoria.com/downloads/200 8%20Research%20World.pdf) I haven't heard a single other copywriter talking about this but it's very powerful stuff! So be the first businessperson on your block to scoop the competition and when you write your marketing copy, include information that talks about: **Balance, Transformations, Journeys, Containers, Connections, Resources and Control.**

14. **Include a call to action**. A visitor has arrived on your site, read your headline and scrolled to the bottom of Page One. What is it you want them to do next? Download your free report? View your weekly specials? Call for a free consultation? If you want to keep the conversation going (and you do!) make it easy for readers to take the next step: but tell them what it is first.

15. **Include some testimonials or third-party endorsements**. But leave it open-ended. Some people don't care what other people think of your product or service — they want to decide for themselves whether you're any good at what you do, and you want to respectfully invite them to do that. So while you might include a quote from a satisfied customer on the one hand, make sure you add in a comment that says, "But you probably want to check it out for yourself and we'd be pleased to answer any questions you have about the effectiveness of our product."

16. **Avoid grammatical mistakes.** Always proof your marketing copy and have someone else read it *before* you go live with it. Typos, spelling mistakes, confusing sentences, and the like, all damage your credibility and — whether you like it or not — they call your professionalism into question. My favourite grammatical reference book is still the Strunk and White classic, "The Elements of Style." You can get a paperback edition on amazon.com for a few dollars or access the online version for free at www.bartleby.com/141.

17. **Use images.** People love pictures, and so do the search engines. One well-placed optimized image of an idea or feeling you would like to convey is still worth 1,000 words.

Don't be discouraged if this all seems daunting at first. Although there is a knack to writing marketing copy it all pretty much turns on whether you know who your perfect customer is, what they need and what you can do to make their life better.

The man who first taught me the tricks of the copywriting trade was a reluctant teacher at best.

He was memorable, however, and his image has stuck with me for decades now, as have many of the others who've had a part in my development as a writer.

Perhaps the best advice The Boss gave me, however, occurred late one evening as we raced to meet yet another impossible deadline. It was the simplest piece of advice imaginable. And it was very, very powerful.

The Boss was tired of giving me detailed directions about phrasing and creativity, colour and benefits. He was tired of my technical questions and my inability to read his mind. He just wanted me to get it:

So, he sat at his desk with his cigarette cradled in his right hand and his favourite pen balanced in his left. He leaned back in his chair and glanced thankfully at the can of beer he had parked neatly beside his ash tray.

He sighed heavily and looked up at the ceiling for a long time, as though asking for just a little more patience, a little more time.

"None of that other stuff matters all that much, Susie," he said finally. "Ya just gotta make it *cook*."

So I did.

The Boss is gone, now, the victim of a heart attack that occurred some years before one might have expected him to leave us. But his advice still lingers, caught between the spark of the future and the dust of the ages.

But go ahead, readers. Make it *cook*.

Action You Can Take Today:

Take a look at some of the writing that represents your business and assess how strong it is from the perspective of what I've outlined above.

You'll want to give special consideration to your web copy, your blog, your company newsletter, but the information I've given in this chapter can apply to any of your marketing documents.

If you feel the copy needs refreshing, hire a writer. My business offers writing services and you can email us at susan@crossmancommunications.com for more information.

You can also do an online search for "marketing copywriter" to find someone in your area, although I find a Skype conversation is often sufficient to obtain the information we need in order to write good copy.

Make sure you ask anyone you hire to write for you for their credentials. Not all writers are experienced at writing marketing copy and it is a special skill.

Chapter Six
A Little More on Writing for the Web

OK, I'm a writer so bear with me while I spend a little more time on writing. I've been doing this for decades and I am continually investing in training that will help me, even at this stage of my career, write better so my clients can achieve the results they seek.

Your content includes a lot more than text, of course, and visuals are a powerful way of connecting with people online. At the same time, words are a crucial component of your online presence and presenting your business and your business proposition in a coherent way depends on how well you can string a sentence together.

Other opportunities probably present in your life for expressing, in writing, what you do and how you do it as well. So is there ever a downside to improving how well you write?

As a writer and editor I see written material at all levels of competency and, as I like to tell the clients who seek my editorial input on their book-writing projects, we are each on our own writing continuum.

I believe it's always possible to improve, and that continued practice and learning is the key to development.

I've provided material for the corporate communications departments of a number of multi-national organizations and have often been impressed by the level of professionalism and capability of employees in these areas of a company; at the same time, I've also heard executives in other departments bemoan the language skills of employees whose main purpose is to do something other than write.

And, as I mentioned earlier in this book, writing is a key skill that relates directly to a company's bottom line: the higher the overall level of literacy in an organization, the more likely that company will be to meet goals, enhance relationships and generate revenue.

Strong communication creates results, and that is true in every form of business correspondence, from simple emails to annual reports. There's no wiggling out of it: a business needs employees who can communicate fluidly and effectively.

I had the great good fortune to hear former CEO of Franklin-Covey — and fervent champion of the English language — Hyrum Smith speak about the importance of clear expression. I mention him here because what he had to say astounded me and it might stir you to action as well.

Smith noted that there are approximately 343,000 words in the English language and he told listeners that Winston Churchill had the highest working vocabulary of any human being ever known, at about 25,000 words.

The average business person, by contrast, has a working vocabulary of 12,000 words. And the average teenager in North America right now has a working vocabulary of 2,300 words.

Shocking, isn't it?

What is the future of our country and our economy if we are not grooming young people to speak and write clearly, comprehensively and persuasively?

While format changes from one type of business document to another, if your job requires you to demonstrate any degree of language facility at all, you might want to keep these ideas in mind when you're developing your next document:

1. Skip the buzz words.

Every industry sector, and probably every company, comes complete with a standard range of terms and phrases that slip off the tongues of people in every department and end up mangling a perfectly good language. For example:

> **Decisioning.** Ugh! A team doesn't meet so they can get busy decisioning. They might make decisions or deliberate, or problem-solve. But they do not decision;

> **Learnings**, as in "There were many learnings in the experience." The proper term is "lessons" or, in a pinch, "takeaways;"

> **Solutionize,** as in, "Together as a team we can solutionize the situation." Pretty please, throw that word out and use the correct one, which is "solve;"

> **Wordsmith, used as a verb,** as in "Melva can go and wordsmith the document and then we'll send it upstairs." I practically stamp my feet in frustration when I hear that one. Melva might well be a wonderful wordsmith but she will be editing that document, not wordsmithing it.

You get the drift: Make it a habit to sniff out unconventional uses of your language and critically ask yourself if they are contributing to a better understanding of your idea, or fogging up the landscape.

I'm all for creativity. But not at the expense of meaning. Especially when you are trying to connect with people who might want to buy what you're selling.

2. Watch out for Redundancies

We tend to default to common usage in a lot of our writing and unfortunately common usage is sometimes sloppy.

I hate to be a tyrant about language but there's no advantage to using more words than necessary to get your point across. They take up more space and occupy more of people's valuable time, so precision is everyone's friend.

Here are a handful of offenders that you might want to eliminate from your writing playbook:

- **Absolutely certain.** Certain already means without doubt. Absolutely doesn't add any value.

- **Added bonus.** A bonus is already something extra so the word "added" isn't necessary.

- **Advance warning.** A warning is already something that happens ahead of an event; the word "advance" doesn't make it happen any earlier.

- **Ask a question**. What else can one ask? An answer? You can't ask something without involving a question so the words "a question" are redundant.

- **Basic essentials.** Essentials are as basic as you can get already; you don't need the adjective!

- **Came at a time when.** When provides the necessary temporal reference to the action of coming; "at a time" is redundant.

- **Close proximity.** Proximity already means close so pick one or the other.

- **Difficult dilemma.** A dilemma is by definition something difficult to resolve so the word "difficult" is unnecessary.

- **Direct confrontation.** A confrontation involves head-to-head conflict and it doesn't get any more direct than that!

- **End result.** A result is already at the end of a process; omit the word "end."

- **Estimated at roughly.** The word "estimate" already tells the reader that the quantity is an approximation; the word "roughly" is unnecessary.

- **Final outcome.** An outcome can't help being final!

- **First began.** A beginning is whatever happened first so that word is unnecessary.

- **Foreign imports.** Imports by their very nature are foreign. Lose the word "foreign."

- **Free gift.** Aren't gifts always free?

- **Major breakthrough.** Isn't a breakthrough intrinsically major? A breakthrough is a significant progress in an effort and the notable nature of the event is implicit.

- **Past history.** History is what happened in the past so ditch the "past!"

- **Plan ahead.** Since planning is what occurs ahead of time anyway we don't need to add in the word "ahead."
- **Protest against.** A protest implies opposition so the word "against" is unnecessary.
- **Repeat again.** To repeat already means to say something again so the word "again" is redundant.
- **Revert back.** Well, we can't exactly revert forward, can we? Ditch the "word back!"
- **Sudden explosion.** If an event occurs gradually it cannot be an explosion; omit the word "sudden."
- **Unexpected surprise.** If a surprise is expected it is not a surprise! Delete "unexpected."
- **Written down.** The word "down" is redundant.

3. Use Detail and Think Big

We know from studies in learning and psychology that some people are adept at big picture thinking and others are absolute maniacs with detail. Great writing incorporates both, but one of the biggest challenges I've seen among my editing clients is the tendency to default to the conceptual at the expense of the detail.

I want to know that a new project will revolutionize product sales at my company, of course.

But tell me why, tell me how and tell me what the end results are going to be!

4. Show, Rather than Tell

This is a key concept for success in the creative writing stratosphere and it's no less important in the business world.

You can tell people how great your program is until you run out of oxygen and they'll actually believe it when you provide them with proof.

Judicious use of statistics, graphs and images, as well as actual case study story-telling, is far more compelling than a mere statement of unproven "fact."

5. Avoid Common Errors

There are a lot of wrong turns you can take in English and a slight deviation from standard practice can affect your credibility and muddle your meaning.

I see a lot of errors in the use of tenses in my work so it's a good idea to invest in some good grammar training if you feel this is not an area of strength for you.

This book is not intended to be a grammar training manual — plenty of other people have tackled that far more effectively than I ever could.

But the following list may help you avoid some of the most common faux-pas I see:

> **Apostrophes.** We only use them to denote the fact that one or more letters are missing (won't, don't, can't, shouldn't, etc.) or to show possession. (Janet's report, Henry's computer).
>
> **Affect vs. Effect.** These ones are tricky! Affect involves a process and effect relates to a result. So you

can say "The movie affected deeply." Or "It takes 15 minutes for the medication to take effect."

Bated breath. Not "baited breath!"

Could of, would of and should of. They are all incorrect! The proper wording is could have, would have and should have.

Edition vs. addition. Edition is about a publication (e.g. the 12th edition of the book, the fourth edition of a magazine). Addition is about adding numbers together.

E.g. vs. i.e. E.g. is the abbreviation of the Latin words, "exempli gratia" (meaning "for example"). We use it this way: "I appreciate the classical musicians, e.g. Bach, Mozart and Handel." I.e. is the abbreviation of the Latin "id est," meaning "that is to say." I would use it this way: "Of all the music available today, I like Bach, Mozart and Handel the best, i.e. I prefer classical music."

Into vs. in to. We can walk into a room or go into a business but we go in to see the dentist.

It's vs. its. It's is the contraction of the words "it is." ("It's raining out!") Its denotes possession ("The robot lifted its hand.")

Me vs. I. "I" functions as the subject of a sentence, the person doing the action. "John and I are going skiing." "Me" is always used with a preposition. "John is coming with me."

Peak, peek and pique. A mountain has a peak, a quick look is a peek and when you are curious it means something has piqued your curiosity.

Then vs. than. "Then" is about time ("I read the news and then I checked the weather."). "Than" is used to make a comparison ("I was less energetic today than you were!")

Ultimate vs. Penultimate. Ultimate is the very last one; penultimate is the second last one. "November is the penultimate month in the year."

A 360 Degree Turn. This implies you are back where you started. A 180 degree turn, by contrast, means you completely reversed direction.

There are plenty more and I suggest that if you're interested you might want to do an online search to learn more of the most common mistakes people make with their writing.

6. Proofread Everything!

I know how easy it is to skip this crucial step in the writing process – we're all busy and many people barely have enough time to develop a rough draft of the project they've been assigned, let alone polish it into practical perfection. That's a formula for linguistic suicide.

The clearer you can be in your communication, the more likely you are to generate the results you seek. Here are a few ideas to make the proofing phase more palatable:

- Start with a "big picture" scan of what you've written. Have you included all the major ideas? Have you left anything out? Do you need to delete any irrelevant information? Is everything in the right place?

- Go through your document and delete any unnecessary words. I've written a lot of newsletter material over the years and sometimes space requirements change partway through a project and I need to cut a 500-word article down to 200. I start by seeing how far I can get by simply tightening up every sentence and trying to replace five words with two or three. It's surprising how easy this is and it often shows me where I've been too wordy (lazy?) in the first place.

- Read the document aloud to catch any spelling mistakes or grammatical errors –your ear may pick them up more readily than your eyes will.

- Take breaks. Sometimes we get so close to our copy that we miss glaring errors or omissions and often that little walk around the block can make a world of difference to our ability to read critically. Often a break of an entire day or three is beneficial as well, so if you can afford the time, always take it.

- Print the document and read it on paper. Much as I am a fan of preserving our trees, studies have shown that the human eye is not always perfectly suited to screen reading, whereas reading printed letters on actual paper is a much easier and accurate way to process information.

- Use spell check. Critically. Spell check is sometimes wrong and the more you learn about the English language, the more confident you can be in deciding whether or not to accept the changes Spellcheck thinks you should make.

7. And What about Writer's Block?

Is there any writing term more famous than "Writer's Block?" It's almost a legendary concept and even after decades of professional writing experience I still have those occasional moments when the words just won't come. They park themselves stubbornly beyond the veil of my accessible reality, nonchalantly filing their nails or humming cheerfully to themselves while I drive myself into an increasing frenzy of frustration.

It becomes something of a game between us: I go grab another cup of coffee. The words stay away. I make a couple of phone calls. The words stay away. I tidy my desk....

If I'm working on a piece of non-fiction or a business-related document, the problem can sometimes be traced to insufficient information.

I tend to over-research almost everything I write so that I can pick and choose from only the very best factual information. So sometimes when Writer's Block hits, I immediately check to see if I need to do a little more research.

At other times, my head is so cluttered with other things that are going on in my life that I simply can't settle down to work. There I sit, hunched over my keyboard hoping to write, when suddenly my mind is ping-ponging at Olympic speed between intruding thoughts: another project, the dog's epilepsy, my recent tax statement, the rabbit's litter training, hopes for an upcoming holiday, the meat I forgot to take out of the freezer for dinner....and who knows what else? It's deadly!

If that happens to you, be kind to yourself. Step. Away. From. The. Desk. Go for a walk. Clear your head.

Ponder. Collect those errant thoughts and words in a nice wicker basket in your head and think about what you want to write about as though it were a cherished friend. Allow ideas and phrases to take over your mind and enjoy the fresh air (or, if you are in a city, the gentle smog).

Let the piece start writing itself in your head. After a decent period of time, say at least half an hour, revisit your computer and start to type. Expand on what you wrote in your head.

It's a good idea to keep a notebook with you at all times, or consistently use the "Notes" function on your mobile device, so you can jot down words and phrases, thoughts and ideas, as they pop into your head at odd times of the day – while you're sitting on a bus, for example, or standing in the grocery line.

Capturing them for later use is actually also a time-saving device as well, since you will gradually build up a library of brilliant expressions that are available to you anytime, anywhere.

Some people like to take a break from their writing before they finish a thought so they can get right back to work as soon as they return.

It's like a kindly kick-start to your writing flow and, of course, once you are in the flow of writing you are usually able to keep going.

These tips might also be helpful:
- Schedule your writing time well
- Stay away from online distractions
- Give yourself a deadline

But this all brings me to another topic, which is the process of writing itself. I've been asked before what the "right" way to do it is and I'm afraid that's a judgement I cannot make. It really shouldn't matter to anyone else whether you're sitting with your laptop at the board room table or perched in a coffee shop near a main intersection in your town. The "right" way for you is the one that brings you the best results.

Personally I need a room where there are no distractions, and that often means getting out of my office where the phone might ring, other projects might call and just a glance around the room might remind me that I need to order another printer cartridge or fill my water jug.

There is a quiet room at my local library where conversation is not allowed and I often lug my laptop over there, plug in my headphones (I listen to Chamber music) and get right down to work.

I also need a long interrupted period of time in order to write smoothly. Trying to fit any half-way decent writing into a spare half hour between meetings does not work for me at all.

But three hours on a Tuesday afternoon does. In fact, I try to keep my weekday afternoons free in order to have those large blocks of time available to write, and that seems to work well for me.

Finally, I need to be rested. If I am over-tired I don't write (or edit) well. Ever. The words swim in front of my eyes and I am capable of reading the same sentence seven or eight times with nary a critical thought in sight.

I'm up by 5:00 a.m. every weekday morning and I often don't get to bed before 11:00 at night.

My days are packed with all the hectic racing that a modern life demands.

I do get tired! But because people pay me to write and edit, there is an integrity issue involved for me: they are not paying for my worst efforts, they are paying for my best.

When I'm tired I conscientiously do the only thing I possibly can do to rectify the matter: I take a nap.

Half an hour of guilt-free napping is usually all it takes to bring my energy back up again and I can resume my writing or editing with renewed efficiency and focus.

Writing is a magical occupation and doing it well is gratifying. But we each need to develop our own way of going about it – what works for me might not necessarily work for you and the point isn't to match someone else's idea of "Right," but rather to get the job done as effectively and gracefully as possible.

Action You Can Take Today:

Start looking at the writing you—and other people in your business — do with an eye to improving it. Pick one of these suggestions, that I've just discussed, every day and filter everything you read and write with it in mind.

Chapter Seven
Your Website

Raise your hand if you love your website.

Actually, whether or not you love your website doesn't matter all that much. What matters is whether or not your *ideal customer* loves your website.

And, as we've seen previously, if you've done some deep breathing and heavy lifting around figuring out your brand, you know who that ideal customer is and what resonates with them. That's the kind of information you can then hand off to your web guy (I'm pretty sure that's an official term) and your content creator so they can cheerfully turn out a website that rocks.

Websites have changed a lot in the last five years and they will continue to change going forward. The pace of evolution is a little frightening, actually, and this is one area where it's tough to stay current.

When I finally decided to take the plunge and invest in my first website, I didn't know anything about websites, other than that it was long past time for my business to have one.

At that time, websites were mostly what we're now calling "brochure" websites – they contained information about your business, much like a brochure would, but *WOW it's on the Internet*!!!

The downside was that most websites weren't all that attractive because the highly technical people in our world held the keys to the internet kingdom and graphic designers were still figuring out how to stake their claim to the wild world of *digital* design.

In fact, that still holds true today: most web designers I meet are technical people who will make your website look as good as they can.

But back in the dawn of my business's internet debut, I wanted an attractive website, one that was visually consistent with my brand, so that when people arrived at my url, thanks to the business card I had given them, they felt like there was a match, that they had found my place of business, and that they felt encouraged to find out more about me.

When there is no visual match between your website and your other branded materials, people will have the unsettling experience of getting to your site and wondering if they're in the wrong place. The mismatch happens primarily at a subconscious level, but the brain reads inconsistency as unreliability and you really don't want people feeling in any way, shape or form that you are unreliable.

You want every step of your relationship with them to confirm a consistent brand experience, and your website is a key part of that process. It needs to look good. Somebody with a strong understanding of the role visual imagery plays in marketing needs to be involved in the design.

Why is that? Why is graphic design so important?

Well, partly because most people are far more visually oriented than textually oriented.

A really good graphic designer will be able to take all of the brand information and persona information that you worked so hard to develop, and translate it into imagery that expresses your company's value proposition to your ideal customers.

Your graphic imagery, which gets condensed into your logo but is present in every one of your sales documents, is a structure for consistently delivering your brand promise to the people with whom you want to do business.

Consistency is always a good thing in marketing. It creates confidence and communicates predictability.

Did you ever wonder why big corporations don't tend to mess with their logos? It's generally because there is a huge amount of brand recognition tied up in a logo and people's understanding of a brand personality is triggered when they look at the logo. It captures emotion and communicates it to the viewer.

Consider the McDonald's Logo. Can you remember a time when it looked any different than it does now? It's red and yellow and has a curvy, happy, sunshiny feel to it, which is completely in line with the image the company offers and the mood it wants to create when people in its target audience think of McDonald's Golden Arches on a red background.

Now consider the Kodak logo, which is also red and yellow, but which strives to serve a different audience with a vastly different product. I remember Kodak's logo on the boxes that held the reels of film my father created with his state-of-the-art Super 8 camera back in the 1960s. As far as I can tell, the logo hasn't changed in decades. But there is a dramatically different feel to the Kodak logo, even though it has pretty much the same colours as the McDonald's logo.

And how about cars? The car companies spend mountains of money on their marketing and for good reason. It's a competitive field. But their logos don't tend to change from year to year either.

Toyota, for example, has a nice silver and red logo – but so does Cadillac: The two companies have very different price points, and we expect a very different product experience from each one. Although these two logos use similar colours, their customers — for whom they no doubt have created personas — have very different values, priorities, spending habits and lives. The logos allow each company to communicate visually to their ideal customers that they're a perfect match.

What is your logo saying about you? And are you carrying your logo's brand promise into all of your marketing materials?

When someone comes to your website, will they experience an immediate match between what they see there and the marketing imagery they saw on your business card, your trade show signage, the brochures you mailed or emailed out, and your newsletter?

Brand promise is communicated with the logo and it should be carried through on the type of font you use, and the design style – is it cluttered and free flowing or spare and highly organized?

Whatever you have determined resonates with your ideal clientele, that style needs to be replicated on every single one of your marketing materials. Ideally you want the same graphic designer doing the work. Consistency is king.

You have mere seconds to grab a website visitor's attention and convince them to stay on your website in order to find out more about you. Your copy might be spectacular, but if it isn't packaged in a well-branded, visually intriguing manner, that visitor will fly off your site and get on to the next one. Does your competitor deserve the business more than you do? Your graphics can help convince them to stay.

Good graphic treatment of your website, altogether, can contribute to:

- Strong brand recognition
- A highly professional reputation
- The symbolic communication of ideas
- The efficient presentation of your information and
- Revenue generation

Really good graphic designers are very special people and they should be a key part of your team. Think of a designer as someone who speaks your customer's language.

You could natter at your ideal customer all day long in the language you yourself speak and hope, vainly, that they will respond. But with just a few whispers, your graphic designer can tell your ideal customer exactly what they need to hear to feel friendly about the idea of having a conversation with you. Which is, after all, the goal of your marketing.

Graphic design involves a lot of emotion and it's communicated through colour, shape, proportion and white space.

A good designer spends a lot of time getting to know their clients and they spend a lot of time staring at the wall, thinking.

They dream. They look at a few design magazines for inspiration. They ponder. They go get another cup of coffee. They call their mothers. They look for their favourite pencil.

They sharpen it. They shut the door to their office. They do a little deep breathing. They lean in to their blank computer screen. And they start to play with ideas.

Graphic design is a highly creative, and yet often very technical process, and the logo, website or brochure that a designer creates is the culmination of years of training, tons of practice, and probably more than a few mistakes.

Different designers tend to have different design styles and some are likely going to be more suitable to your business and your clientele than others.

But you want a designer involved, at the very least, in the creation or updating of your logo, and the standardization of your brochures, letterhead, business card and signage.

I love it when a designer is involved in the creation of a website, but not all web design companies will pay the extra freight of hiring a graphic designer who understands visual communication exceedingly well, *and* who gets the technical side of web development.

Some graphic designers have made the leap into the technical side of web design but be aware that there are distinct skill sets involved in the visual and technical aspects of web design and you want a website, ideally, that leverages both priorities.

The Technical Aspect of a Website:

Which brings us to the techie stuff. Although my first exciting and visually appealing website had been put together by a wonderful graphic designer who understood my brand and my service offer well, it was not designed to attract the attention of web crawlers, those creepy bots that prowl the outer reaches of Web World snooping on innocent websites and deciding if they are worthy of Page One ranking.

I am a web design company's worst nightmare. I know exactly what I want my new website to look like and, with a background in art direction, I am alert to the tiny little details that impair visual appeal.

I also have high expectations of the architecture and search engine data that I want my website to feature.

And I'm a small business: I don't want to pay the proverbial arm and leg for great results.

With my fourth website rolling up to the launching pad, and almost a decade spent learning how to differentiate one kind of web development company from another, I'm wary of a web design company that claims to be all things to all people.

A good technically-oriented web designer loves playing with code, the behind-the-scenes information that communicates all kinds of information to the web crawlers to induce them to look favourably on your site.

They understand metadata and tagging and categories and keywords.

They care about building a site that the search engines love.

And they stay abreast of the changes in search engine protocol so that when Google changes its algorithm, for example, they can implement the kinds of technical modifications that will maximize your chances of being found online.

If you're really lucky, your web designer will also be *au courant* with conversion architecture and strategy so that all those new visitors are funnelled into a deeper sales-oriented relationship with you.

Online search is a complex topic but suffice for now to say that your website is an important part of your online "findability."

And in a perfect world, or in a fortunate moment, you will find yourself a web designer who can do it all.

But What's a Website Supposed to Do for You?

A website can cost anywhere from $2,000 to $50,000 (and more) so, for most businesses, it's a substantial expense.

And the task of renovating an existing website requires precious time – you need to go through the arduous process of selecting a website provider, and be available to guide the process of developing the new website according to your vision for the business.

Here's what you want that website to accomplish:

1. Stake your claim to your online real estate. If you don't have a website you have a much harder time building the kind of presence that supports findability. It can still be done. But if you want to maintain a competitive position among the dozens or hundreds of companies that do what you do around the world, you have to have a website.

2. Leave a positive impression. When people arrive at your website you want them to immediately feel good about your company. If they're there because one of your sales reps handed them a business card that

directed them to your website, the website's job is to confirm the positive vibe that's already been created.

3. Tell your potential customers what you do. Even when your office is closed. You need a place to send people where they can learn about your business 24/7. In the old days, we gave out brochures, and that's still a good idea. But the world has gone online and if you're not presenting yourself in a powerful way in a format that is convenient and agreeable to your customers, then you miss the opportunity to start a conversation with them that might lead to a sale.

4. If they found you through an online search, the same thing applies: the website will need to leave a positive first impression and be consistent with your other branding materials. Either way, you want that website to draw people into a further engagement with you. It needs to look clean and it needs to be easy to navigate. Showcase your products or services. A manufacturing company usually has more to show than a service-oriented business and you want to get images of your products up on your website so people have something to look at. Images are good, videos are even better. Show that equipment in action!

5. Differentiate your product or service and gain credibility. Your website needs to state your value proposition and demonstrate to visitors what it is about what you do that is more effective, less expensive, more efficient, safer, smarter, or in any way better than your competitors.

6. Introduce your key people. Nice colour photos of the people who are in positions of authority or responsibility in your company, with a well-written bio, go a long way to demonstrating to visitors that the people in your company care and that they deserve their confidence.

7. Create opportunities for lead generation and communication. The point of any web marketing is to generate leads that might turn a visitor into a customer. You can do this by giving them an opportunity to sign up for your "IFO" (Irresistible Free Offer) – for an eBook, template or guide to something that is relevant to them. You can also invite them to sign up for your blog or newsletter. The people who are most interested in your product or service will sign up for your offer, and you can follow up with them to bring them closer to a sale.

8. Support your customers. Many businesses create a customer portal on their website that allows their customers to log-in and obtain product updates or other information that is valuable to them. They use the portal to update records relevant to the product or service you offer, seek support or find solutions to problems they're having.

9. Information distribution. Your website allows you to host information about your company above and beyond your web copy. Press releases. Product sheets. Case studies. Articles. Posting new content generates more search engine findability and teaches your ideal customers more about how you can solve their problems.

Of course, all of the above relies on lots of solid, well-written, visually attractive content: the words and images you use to communicate to your ideal customers matter.

You want to make sure that you have a strategy for the judicious addition of content to your website: it anchors all of your online marketing efforts.

Everything else you do online involves funnelling people to your website where they can find out more about your business and engage with you on some level.

Calls to Action

You need "Calls to Action," which are things you want your visitors to do next, like pick up the phone, download your free whitepaper, email you for more information, watch your free video series, etc.

I personally feel that the trend to producing websites where the home pages are nothing but clickable images with one or three words on them is appalling.

I land on those sites and don't have a clue what product or service is being sold — there is no context to frame my pain or explain, from a "big picture" perspective what exactly this company does or why I should care.

Why, indeed, should I click?

So even if your website is a digital miracle that uses the best technology money can buy, make sure it provides some context for your visitors.

Make sure it puts them in the story.

Action You Can Take Today:

Shop your website. Pretending you are a potential customer, visit every page of your website and rank yourself from 1 to 10 on the criteria I've listed below. A "10" means "Yup, nailed it" and a "1" means "Help!":

- Visual appeal

- Corporate branding: is this clearly about *your* company? If you took out the logo could it be about anyone in your industry?

- Balance between talking about your products and services and addressing how much they address your customers and their needs? We're aiming for a 40-60 split in favour of the customer.

- Features versus the benefits of your products and services. Does your site merely *describe* them or does it *explain* what your products will actually do for people.

- Do you have "Calls to Action" on every page? (Call or email us for more information, download our checklist or guidebook, book a free consultation, etc.)

- People. You want visitors to see some.

- Links. Do they all work?

Scores:
50-70   You're doing OK
35-50   You need help
<35   Oh dear.

Chapter Eight:
Your Blog

Most of the industrial companies I work with have not, at the outset, jumped into the world of blogging and I think there's a lot of mystery about blogging and how to do it that often keeps people out of that particular online pool.

I get it. You don't want to waste valuable company time and resources on something that doesn't seem to draw a straight line to revenue and, if you aren't sure how to go about doing it to begin with, then it doesn't make a whole lot of sense.

When I began blogging about five years ago I embraced the concept with a ton of enthusiasm and a great deal of hope.

I'm a professional writer with decades of experience – writing is easy for me and it's something I love to do. I felt I had lots to say about web writing and marketing and it's fun for me to share. I am rarely shy. I have no end of ideas for what I could be writing about.

So, I embraced blogging confidently, and with something akin to religious zeal, and pumped out a weekly blog that was a lot of fun to create and, as I mentioned earlier in the book, my efforts delivered no results at all.

For six months.

I was puzzled and discouraged. How can all that writing not generate *some* results? Especially after six months of trying?!

And, actually, it probably was delivering *some* results from a search engine optimization perspective simply because I was consistently posting fresh content to my website, which is something for which the search engines will dole out Crawler Love.

But in terms of providing my target market with information that positioned me well, it was an absolute fail.

I had completely neglected to develop a persona for my copywriting at that point and I didn't have an editorial schedule that laid out, in an organized fashion, the problems my ideal customers were dealing with and how I might help them solve them.

In other words, my writing had been all about me. What *I* wanted to write about. What *I* thought was important. What *I* was interested in exploring. Bring on the gong!

Your blog, like almost every other morsel of online content, **is not always about you**. It's about your ideal customers and how you serve them. It can be highly informational – as long as it isn't just another long list of blather about how great your company is. Nobody wants to read that.

You want to provide information that might trigger in your ideal customers a niggling desire to either pick up the phone and give you a call or send you an email to start an exchange about how you can help them.

If all you do is write about what you do and how you do it, nobody is going to think you are aware of a universe outside your front reception area, let alone that you care about your customers or could maybe even help them with the problems they are having.

Few, if any, of my clients can pull off a weekly blog all be themselves, let alone the two-to-three times a week that many experts recommend. If I were writing three blogs a week for my own business I would soon

a) drop from exhaustion because a well-written blog takes a lot of time and energy. Creating three well-written blogs every week would mean I was devoting an inordinate amount of time I don't have to delivering great content. And

b) I would possibly go out of business because fostering a blog takes a lot of time and energy...if I had to blog three times a week I would not be devoting my resources to serving my clients and they would soon tire of waiting for me to respond to *their* needs.

My clients are similarly pressed for time as well, and paying me to blog three times a week on their behalf would run up a sizable bill very quickly.

Yes, they can go to a site like Fivr or Elance and hire someone for $10 a page to crank out masses of inexpensive "professionally written" blog copy. But, no, it will not likely strike to the heart of what makes my client incredible.

One of my clients was buying blog copy from a company that was using cheap writing labour from a crowdsourcing site.

My client assumed he was paying for quality content and, at $100 a pop, he felt he should be getting some good stuff.

He assumed all was well and, being an incredibly busy guy, he wasn't paying close attention to what was being posted on his behalf.

When I arrived on the scene and started to take a close look at his online content, it was apparent that he was not well served by the arrangement: the blogs were full of spelling and grammatical errors, they contained links to offsite pages that no longer existed, other service providers in his field had been sold the identical blog, and the blogs referred to geographical locations his business did not serve.

It was a disaster and pointed to the fact that cheap, plentiful blogs are not necessarily the way to go.

So for most of my clients, I recommend one blog every two weeks to start. It's not ideal — once a week is better — but it's still often enough to generate some search engine interest while serving customers with the understanding that you have important things to say and you are saying them.

Sometimes, my clients will write the blogs themselves and we'll provide some good editing to make sure they're pulling readers in a useful direction; other times, when we know our clients well, we will originate the blogs and our clients will fine tune them.

A blog is an excellent way for a company to stay in touch with its former, current and prospective customers.

It keeps the company name front and centre with its target audience and, properly constructed, will also position company representatives as powerful and engaging leaders — and thought leaders — in their field. In order to maximize the benefits of a blog (from both a customer ***and*** search engine perspective), it must be produced consistently as a value-driven proposition that is focused on the needs and interests of customers.

Many business owners today have a general and uneasy feeling that they should be blogging but reliable information on the contextual issues around a blog is rare.

It's important to understand why blogging is worth the expense and, just as important, to understand, at the outset, that bottom-line results are dependent upon consistency over time.

Maintaining a commitment to blogging once the project has begun is key. Three blog postings will not deliver the kind of results that is likely to be evident after 30, for example.

So Why Is Blogging Valuable?

1. Blogging establishes you and your company as experts in your field just by virtue of the fact that you are blogging. This is a concept along the lines of famed communicator Marshall McLuhan's contention that "the medium is the message."

2. A blog gives you the chance to showcase your employees' skills, talents and knowledge, building greater credibility with your audience. Telling the stories of how your employees have solved problems and delivered results to your customers positions you all as caring experts who are willing and able to "go the extra mile" for your customers.

3. It is a tool for developing greater rapport with your existing client base. Marketing is all about giving your ideal customers the information they need so that they will know, like and trust you enough to want to start a conversation that might lead to a sale. Sharing more about what you do and how you do it in a blog can help do just that.

4. It is a tool for retaining existing clients and extending your client base. It helps remind people how great it is to work with you.

5. It is a means of protecting market share. If your competition isn't blogging, you own the field; if they are blogging, you have an opportunity to position yourself in a way that plays to your strengths and subtly highlights the deficiencies of competitors. Gently and with grace.

6. It gives you a mechanism for educating your clients and prospects

7. Like all social media, a blog is a chance to create a footprint for your organization that is larger than you might otherwise enjoy. It's an engaging way to broaden your "social media real estate" holdings.

8. It is a relatively inexpensive form of marketing.

9. It's a chance to voice concerns over issues in your field that disturb you. Is the government talking about introducing legislation that you feel will negatively affect your customers? Are there trends in how your product or service is being viewed or restricted that you feel are dangerous? You can talk about them freely, with an eye on customer value, in your blog.

10. It increases your company's search engine results, *especially* if you optimize for your key words and invite engagement. The search engines love fresh content and reward businesses that produce it regularly.

11. It is an important tool for funneling people to your website where they can check you out in more detail and, hopefully, strengthen their interest in

buying from you. And, of course, that means your blog needs to be sited on your website where people can click easily from the blog to other areas of the site.

12. It helps funnel people to your website so they can deepen their interest in doing business with you

As I mentioned earlier, different experts have different approaches to blogging.

As for those who claim that it is imperative that a business post new blog content at least three times a week, well, yeah. Great thought. Not too practical for most companies.

If you're in a fast-changing business, there may be ample important information that would merit blogging so frequently.

If you have a dedicated core of employees who know the business well and love to write, then you might be able to pull it off. If you have someone internally who is willing and able to take on responsibility for coordinating and posting blogs regularly, so much the better.

But posting new blogs three times a week requires an awful lot of content and increases the cost of a blogging program substantially.

And, unless your blog content is consistently powerful, you risk diluting your audience's interest in what you have to say.

A more realistic goal is to blog often enough to establish a track record of doing it while building an archive of interesting articles; as I mentioned above, twice a month for starters will do the trick nicely, especially if you are publishing other quality content as well.

Knowledge of and comfort with blogging is something that grows over time.

Your blogging strategy will evolve – what feels right and comfortable in the beginning will give way to other ideas and opportunities for informing your client base about important issues and understandings you feel would benefit them.

It's important to be flexible and it's important to include calls to action in each blog posting.

What Should That Blog Look Like?
I generally recommend a bi-weekly 400-500-word blog focusing on specific topics of relevance to your customers.

You want to start by developing a roster of blog topics that cover the schedule for the forthcoming year: that represents 26 opportunities to position your company as the hands-down customer-focused experts in your field. Anywhere in the world.

This is an opportunity to go into more detail about:

- Product information
- Industry information
- Internal culture
- Values
- History
- Recruiting processes
- Details on changes within the company

- Information about any legislation that might be relevant to your customers

- Events (such as trade show participation, or any upcoming customer informational webinars)

- R&D (generally speaking)

- Q&As about what it's like to work with your company

- Responsiveness to customer demand

- Approach to customer service

- Other information of relevance to your customers. What do they need to know in order to choose your company over your competitors? What do they want to know? How can you provide information that makes a difference in their lives?

Potential blog topics are everywhere in your company and it just takes a bit of imagination to uncover them.

For example, I was interviewing the solutions advisor for one of my clients recently for a case study I was writing.

As we talked about the project, I realized that the communications process my client had developed for the implementations they conducted was very sophisticated and completely customer focused. *That* was a perfect blog topic!

What Does it Take to Make a Blog Happen?

This is an editorial process much like newspapers followed back in the day when I was proud to be in journalism. It isn't difficult but it does require some forethought and some solid organization.

You could easily implement a similar process in your company and to show you how it works, I thought I'd share the process I generally follow with clients. I'll use the experience of my client, "Jim," (not his real name) to show you how it works.

Jim is the CEO of a business in the Greater Toronto Area and he and his team provide a service in highly competitive field.

None of his competitors did blogging or really did much of anything online, which is not unusual in the manufacturing field these days.

So he had a huge opportunity to differentiate his company in his niche.

Jim was concerned about the fact that he had not focused on expanding his business's online presence and we discussed a number of options for doing so.

Budgets were tight and he was nervous. I thought a blog would represent a good first step for him — a way to get started with content marketing that wouldn't take up too much of his time.

Here's how we went about it:

1. **Step One: Brainstorming.** Jim and I met one frosty morning in late November when the Canadian winter was threatening its worst. Because I had already written new website content, I already had a good handle on who Jim's customers were, and what challenges they faced. In fact, we had developed a customer persona. We sat together for an hour or so and did some brainstorming around the kind of problems Jim's customer's face and how, specifically, Jim's business solves those problems. I don't always meet face-to-face with my customers, by the way. Some of them are too far away from my location to make it practical for us to get together. In those cases, we meet by Skype or telephone.

2. **Step Two: Creating an Editorial Calendar.** I next then took all of the information I had gathered from my conversation with Jim and created an editorial calendar for the blogging program. It listed the top six problems Jim's customers face and it itemized three solutions Jim's company provides for each. (See below) It also assigned publication dates for each blog.

3. **Step Three: Approval.** I sent the editorial calendar to Jim for his approval. He and his General Manager were working together on the project so they both took a look at what we were proposing. They didn't do much tweaking but they did make a few adjustments that they felt made the calendar more targeted and accurate.

4. **Step Four: First blogs.** We went ahead and drafted the first five blogs, based on information we already had about Jim and his company. That got us set up for a couple of months into the future and it meant we didn't have to panic about whether or not we were going to meet our deadlines.

5. **Step Five: Flexibility.** Jim has become very excited about his company blog. Although we meet every couple of months so I can gather the information I need for the next four or five blogs in the lineup, he frequently shoots me an email to say "Hey, what about doing a blog about 'X'." Sometimes there is a time-sensitive aspect to the topics he wants us to write about, in which case we do a quick refocus, I contact him for information, we converse (or sometimes just exchange emails, if his schedule is too packed to meet with me directly), and then I draft a blog and send it back to him for review and approval.

Some of my clients prefer to produce their blogs internally, in which case we develop the editorial calendar together and my task is to simply edit the completed blogs for spelling, grammar, customer focus and common sense.

The editorial calendar keeps everybody focused and provides a benchmark for knowing if the project is on task. It also gives us all an easy way to determine if we have covered a great topic in the past.

Whether you produce a blog internally or outsource it, you need to have a clear approvals process in place.

Generally speaking, the fewer people involved in the project the better, since committees slow things down and risk delaying the posting of the content.

The Benefits of Blogging

Jim's blog has been rolling for less than a year but he has already experienced some benefits from the program, specifically:

- More visits to his website

- Greater brand recognition – website visitors are reading his blog, which we know from looking at his Google Analytics statistics, and the messages they see in the blogs are consistent with the messaging elsewhere in Jim's marketing material (his company website, his customer brochures and, soon, his company newsletter)

- A consistent opportunity for customers and potential customers to connect with Jim's company. Jim and his general manager both get email feedback from customers and non-customers alike saying they liked the previous post – which gives them opportunities for conversations focused on customer attraction and retention.

- Jim is enjoying the opportunity to share more about the qualities that make his business extraordinary

- The blog is contributing to stronger search engine results

- Jim's salespeople are able to point customers and prospects to blog topics that relate to issues they are dealing with in their own businesses, thus positioning Jim's company as a valuable resource for providing solid assistance

Sample Blog Topic Templates

Here's an idea – presented in the following Sample Blog Topic Templates – of how we determine blog topics. Using charts such as these, with key headings will help you organize your topics and your thoughts.

This way of looking at it is pretty formal, and we will flesh out the topics with blog posts that are more community or industry oriented as well.

So please utilize the Sample Blog Topic Templates that appear in the next couples of pages to effectively develop some highly effective blogs that really speak to your audience.

Just use the key headings: Your Customers Care or Need to know About: (fill in blank space); Why is this Topic Important? (fill in blank space); What *Specifically* Readers Need to Know; etc. – and before you know it you'll have the topic and framework of your blog in place.

It then becomes a matter of adding detail and content and helpful advice – so please turn to these charts – and let's get started on doing some truly effective blogging.

SAMPLE BLOG TOPIC TEMPLATE/1:

Your Customers Care About or Need to Know About:	Why This Topic is Important:	What *Specifically* Readers need to know:	How Your Company Solves a Problem or Promotes a Solution:	Implications affecting readers' quality of life:
1.	a) b) c)	a) b) c)	a) b) c)	
2.	a) b) c)	a) b) c)	a) b) c)	
3.	a) b) c)	a) b) c)	a) b) c)	

SAMPLE BLOG TOPIC TEMPLATE/2:

Your Customers Care About or Need to Know About:	Why This Topic is Important:	What Specifically Readers need to know:	How Your Company Solves a Problem/ Promotes Solutions:	Implications affecting readers' quality of life:
4.	a) b) c)	a) b) c)	a) b) c)	
5.	a) b) c)	a) b) c)	a) b) c)	
6.	a) b) c)	a) b) c)	a) b) c)	

It's important to stay on track with blog posting. My clients are all extremely busy people and they juggle many priorities. But having a sense of when their deadlines are helps them make sure they deal with the content in a timely fashion.

Let's face it, no small children will be hurt if we are a day late getting the blog up on the website. But I like to have — and hit — my deadlines because consistency is akin to reliability and we want the messages about our clients to support a reputation for reliability.

And, of course, a blog represents more opportunities to start conversations that might lead to a sale.

Make sure you include a "Call to Action" in your blog. This might be an invitation to call your sales team, download your free check list, email your sales team for more information, or sign up for your company newsletter. The idea is to get your blog readers to do something – again, you're trying to start conversations that might lead to a sale.

A lot of people struggle with writing and I like to share a template I learned along the way that simplifies it enormously. It's called the 4-Mat system. It was developed by Harvard University researcher Dr. Bernice McCarthy, who researched and studied audience engagement. I use it for almost everything I write and here's how it works:

We all filter the world around us differently and that means different people need different information at different times in order to process what you're telling them, and in order to engage effectively with your content.

Dr. McCarthy studied thousands of people and determined that if you want to present information in a way that maximizes your chance to engage everybody who might be looking at your information, then you need to do it in a certain order.

Some people are most interested in WHY something is important and if you don't tell them why they should pay attention to what you are offering first, then they will tune out.

Other people want to know WHAT your topic is about. Although they will sit patiently through an explanation of why it's important, if they don't get the "What" information next, then they will tune out.

Still other people want to know HOW something works. And, again, they will plod through the why and what information but if they don't get the How information next, then THEY will tune out.

And, finally, there is a group of people who want to know THE IMPLICATIONS, or the results, of what you're telling them about.

They will listen to why, what and how it all works, but you really need to full circle them to what it makes possible in the world in order for them to truly feel served by your information .

So whenever I write anything, I start with those four headings:

WHY
WHAT
HOW
IMPLICATIONS

And I put relevant point form notes under each heading.

Once I have all the information written down in the right place, I organize each point into a logical order, and then I start writing. I add in an introduction and a conclusion and then I'm good to go!

And What Can You Expect From Blogging?

The short answer: almost anything!

Although we all want people to comment on our blog posts a positive comment doesn't mean those people are going to do business with you. (Yet!)

As long as any comments are positive, they do provide social proof that you are standing at the helm of a great company.

If your blog is sited on your website, by the way, you have the authority to determine which comments you show the world and which ones you hide.

Spammers often crawl the web looking for blogs where they can leave "comments" that are actually garbled instructions to go visit someone else's website. You want to delete those ones from the back end of the site. The good ones can stay!

You might not, in fact, ever hear from anyone about how great your blogs are, or how wonderful your business is.

But what you can do is track how many visitors your blog is getting through Google Analytics or some other analytics program.

You'll find, over time, that some blogs get more visitors than others, and then you can use that information to create more blogs that are like the ones that get more visits.

You want to be linking to your blogs, by the way, through your social media platforms.

The idea of almost all online marketing is to funnel visitors to your website where you have the opportunity to lead them into a conversation that might result in a sale.

Your blogs represent a wonderful opportunity to share information about the kinds of things that make your company special, and you can also reference products or services your company offers in your blog, and link to them, so your visitors have the chance to explore what your company offers.

You can also track results from the calls to action you put in your blog. If you develop a free white paper for site visitors to download and only promote it through your blog, you will know that people are reading your blog and taking action by how many downloads you're getting.

Blogging does take time and, although the results might not be immediately obvious, it's a key part of your content marketing strategy and probably the first component you should consider implementing, if you haven't already jumped in.

This can be as much a branding tool as anything and it's sometimes a "slow converter."

As we know, many people use the web to shop slowly – they visit various sites, research what's out there, think about what they're after, compare, consider and, finally, take action by picking up the phone or sending an email.

It may take some time for people to discover your blog and begin thinking of it as a destination – but the more valuable information you provide in your blog the more interested people will be in returning to your blog.

The old wisdom about marketing still holds: it can take 13-15 impressions before people are ready to make a purchase; consistency counts.

Don't be discouraged if your following builds slowly – it's quietly positioning your business as a reliable source of wisdom, and consistency will pay off eventually.

WRITING TEMPLATE FOR BLOG POSTS:

Blog Topic: _____	
Why is this Important to your Audience? Why do they need to know this information?	
What do they need to know?	
How can your information help them or how does your idea work?	
What are the implications of your information for your audience?	

Action You Can Take Today:

Ready to blog? Then what are you waiting for?!

Assign someone in your organization the task of starting your blog and pick a deadline right now for when you want to see that first blog post up on your website.

You will probably need to contact your webmaster for assistance with adding a blogging module or blog page to your site.

But while they are getting that set up, use the templates provided above to guide you through developing your own blog outline and editorial schedule, and rough out a blog post using the 4-Mat template I've shared in this chapter.

If you feel you need assistance with any of the above, please reach out to Crossman Communications at: susan@crossmancommunications.com.

Chapter Nine
Your Company Newsletter

A newsletter is a pivotal way for a company to stay in touch with its current, former and prospective customers while contributing to the building of a community that looks to the company for leadership and support.

It keeps your company name front and centre with your target audience and, properly constructed, it positions you as a powerful and engaging leader in your field.

Despite all that, many businesses don't have one.

One of my clients had toyed with the idea of a newsletter in the past but, much as they wanted a way to stay in touch with their customers, they were never able to pull it together consistently. And, until my team and I came along, they didn't have the "people" resources to lead the charge either.

The executives of this company are brilliant people and they manufacture a number of products and services in the high-tech sector. The company has been around for more than a quarter of a century and it's very cheerfully looking ahead to its next $10-million milestone. Its North American offices cover all major time zones and it has an aggressive sales strategy that's being carried out by a team of extraordinary salespeople.

What they didn't have was a vehicle for consistently telling the people in their customer database – more than 5,000 people — about the great things that are on at the company.

If you are in business on the planet today with any hope of growing your bottom line, you need to develop a company newsletter. It is a powerful tool for retaining customers and encouraging them to a) do more business with you and b) tell *other* people that they should do business with you, too.

Customer retention is a critical issue today and there are a lot of statistics available online that support the idea that we should all be spending more on the project.

According to the Content Marketing Institute, increasing customer retention rates by 5% increases a company's profit by anywhere between 25% and 95%. And, what's more, increasing customer retention rates by 10% results in a 30% increase in the *value* of the company.

(http://www.cmo.com/articles/2013/7/18/customer_retention.html)

Here are some other interesting statistics that point to the value of increasing your customer retention rates:

- 68% of customers will leave you if they perceive you to be indifferent to them
- A 5% increase in customer retention can increase business by 25-125%
- Repeat customers spend 33% more than new customers

(Source: http://www.slideshare.net/custthermometer/22-customer-retention-stats)

And it's long been known in marketing circles that it costs a lot more to acquire a new customer than it does to retain one. I've seen and heard statistics ranging from five to 30 times more. And, of course, we all know that whether a customer is satisfied with your product or service or not, they are going to tell other people. It's worth the effort to keep them on board, and a newsletter can help you do that. Why else would you consider investing in a newsletter? Think about this – a newsletter can:

- increase lead generation opportunities
- provide opportunities for cross selling
- help solidify your relationships with your customers
- remind customers how to get in touch with you – and why they might want to
- support your other marketing efforts
- provide measurable results, particularly if you send it out via an email provider and post it to your website
- increase your online visibility in general
- communicate your company's unique strengths and attributes
- tell the stories that demonstrate your company's values and culture
- differentiate your company from others in its niche
- help your customers and prospective customers find you more easily online
- help people form positive opinions about your company's customer service, creativity and product performance
- know and understand that you have a sound business capability, an outstanding hands-on skill set and strong leadership
- feel inspired by the example you set for other companies in your niche

In other words, a newsletter allows your business the opportunity to give prospective customers reasons to trust you, and do business with you.

As a business owner I get the reluctance many business owners feel when it comes to spending money on something that doesn't appear to have a direct line-of-sight to new revenue.

If you're bidding on a contract you can quantify all of the costs involved in getting your sales people in front of the decision-makers and you know how big the contract is and how much profit is likely to come out of it. That calculation is a little harder to make with a newsletter or, indeed, with any other content marketing initiatives.

I address this in a little more detail in my chapter on measurement, but for the moment I invite you to look at the cost of setting up your newsletter as an investment. Your content marketing initiatives all work to form a matrix of "convincer strategies" that together draw your ideal customers to your sales people so they can What? Have the conversations that might lead to a sale. More conversations = more sales.

What Might a Newsletter Project Look Like?

A newsletter must be consistently produced, value-driven, and focused on the needs and interests of your customers; it must also include calls to action so readers are clear about opportunities for finding out more about your company's products and services.

A call to action (CTA) might be anything from "download our free checklist" to "call our sales hotline to book your free half-hour consultation."

You're probably already receiving e-newsletters from some of the companies with which you do business. I've heard more than my fair share of clients complain that they don't read all of those newsletters that arrive in their inbox. And there's a whole other conversation we could have about Outlook and spam filters.

I don't read all of those newsletters either. But they show up regularly and they bring those companies' names directly to my computer where I will see them at one point or another. Just the name can be enough sometimes: Even if I don't read the newsletter, I'm reminded of the company.

Every now and then I open one of those newsletters. Every now and then I click on an article and end up on that company's website.

I might not buy anything at that point. But the process will continue repeating. And after a while, if I have identified a need or if the company whose newsletters I'm receiving identify one for me, I just might start a conversation. In fact, I have done that before. And ended up making a purchase. But it didn't happen overnight.

Bear in mind that if I'm really not interested in a company that is sending me newsletters, I will unsubscribe. And so will the people you are not here to serve. The ones who aren't all that bothered by your newsletter, or who just might be interested Some Day, are going to cheerfully delete the emails unopened, and stay on your emailing list. They are at least showing, by their behaviour, that they are not averse to communicating with you.

While each of the newsletters you receive are no doubt unique, they probably share some of the same characteristics.

Here's what you will probably notice about the newsletters you are already receiving from other companies:

1. **They arrive in your inbox as email messages.** The company sending the newsletter (or their subcontractor) writes the articles, loads them into a predetermined email format, and sends it to a list of people, one of whom is you. The process is quite a lot more technical than that, but that's the gist of it. Ideally, they have also posted the newsletter to their website as well, in order to get as much online mileage out of the effort as possible. And, depending on the format, they can also create a printed copy of the newsletter to give out to people at trade shows or during sales calls.

2. **Each edition of the newsletter follows the same visual layout and benefits from the same graphic treatment**. (Remember our little chat about branding back in Chapter Four?) Visual consistency equates to reliability – you don't want to come up with a new "look" for your newsletter every issue.

3. **The newsletter is delivered to your inbox regularly.** The most common schedules are once a quarter, once every second month or once a month. Scheduling consistency equates to reliability. If you have one newsletter ever five months (or so), it's almost not worth the effort. You want to send out your newsletter often enough that people start to expect it. And, by the way, there are email delivery services that offer to manage your email lists and help you track results at the push of a button. You don't have to set up a separate infrastructure internally in order to make this happen.

4. **The newsletter shares actual news.** A newsletter is not just an opportunity to hammer the recipients into spending money with you. It tells about what's going on in your organization and shares a little more about your company culture so people get an idea of what to expect from a relationship with you.

I personally prefer to get my clients onto a monthly newsletter schedule, with each edition of the newsletter carrying half a dozen or more short articles that position the company as experts in their field.

We tend to link back to other areas of the website where we've previously posted full articles about the topic at hand so people can find out more about the issues they find most interesting.

While a blog gives us a chance to show potential customers more about a client's cultural strengths (values, leadership, customer focus, etc.) the newsletter tends to provide nuts and bolts information about what is actually going on at the company.

And, again, we craft each edition of a newsletter to target the true information potential customers need to read in order to build a stronger sense of how my clients can easily solve their problems and make their business better.

Here are some of the subjects your newsletter articles might focus on:

- Existing products and services
- New products and services
- Events (such as trade show participation, upcoming customer informational webinars etc.)

- Maintenance programs

- Statistics relating to your industry and what that means for your customers

- Other articles of relevance to customers and potential customers (What do they need to know? What do they want to know? How can you make their business better?)

- Members of the executive team – who they are and what they do

I tend to be highly procedural in almost everything I do (I sometimes even use a process for thinking more creatively!) and I find that newsletters likewise work best if you can create a consistent process around their production.

When I'm working with a newsletter client I usually start with a discussion around who our target audience is and what results we want. (Remember that bit about your customer Persona? Here's another place where it's important!)

I also recommend my clients take a look at newsletters they're already receiving and collect several whose format they like.

While it's most important that your customers like the newsletter, you also need to feel proud of your efforts.

Having a template to follow makes it easier for your Newsletter Construction Crew.

By the way, you will have noticed by now that content marketing can rely heavily on written material.

Make sure that any writer you hire asks good questions and writes in a straightforward style. You want any writing done on your behalf to be straightforward and free of lingo and technical terms that your customers might not know or understand. You aren't writing to impress people, you are writing to connect with people. That requires some thought about how people are going to receive your information. And good, clear writing!

More on the Process:

Everybody develops their own way of doing things but I've been writing newsletters for more than 25 years (which surprises even me) and I've developed a process that works quite well.

Here are some suggestions:

1. Set out an editorial calendar to lay out a production schedule that aligns with your promotional opportunities for the coming year. I like to have a theme for each issue of a client newsletter and if your business is seasonal in any way, you can readily develop a theme for each issue that relates to the issues that are relevant in your business at specific times of the year.

2. Book regular planning meetings between your key team members and the person who is going to actually create each issue of the newsletter. Your writer needs to have access to current information and is probably going to have questions about how things work. The members of your executive team will probably want customers to know about specific issues or products. So great internal communication is key to making sure the newsletter serves its purpose.

3. Establish a content funnelling system so that your writer has a reliable process for collecting content for each article in each edition of the newsletter. And don't forget about images! While you can purchase images from online sites, it's less expensive and more effective if you can use good quality images that relate to your company, product line or industry. You want at least one graphic for on every newsletter article. Who collects the images in your company and how can your newsletter Lead get their hands on them?

4. Develop a clear and consistent approvals channel so there are no delays in finalizing and posting content.

5. Make a decision around how the newsletter is going to be distributed. Is it going to be available only on the company's website? If so, will it be available as a web page or as a PDF that people can easily print and copy? Are you going to distribute it in PDF form to salespeople so they can send it to their key contacts? Are you going to email it from head office to all of your customers?

6. Develop and/or modify an email channel so you can send the newsletter to your customer database. Numerous companies offer automated email services and there are advantages and disadvantages to each one. Check out Constant Contact, Mail Chimp and Infusionsoft and see if any of them resonate with you.

7. Determine who is going to take primary responsibility for ensuring that the newsletter gets published. Your people are busy. Is someone going to be able to add this in to their workload or do you need to hire it out?

8. Determine where you are going to funnel leads that the newsletter generates. Usually it's sales@xyzcompany.com and one salesperson is assigned to monitor that email address and pick up on any leads generated.

If you're using an email service like Mail Chimp you can easily track how many people are reading your newsletter and what sections they liked best.

That allows you to duplicate that type of article or topic in a future edition of the newsletter so you can keep interest and visits to your website high.

Newsletter "Must-Haves":

- Calls to action
- Links to your website
- Your contact information
- Links to your social media sites
- A newsletter sign-up form that's located on your website
- Your company logo
- A link in the email version of your newsletter to the web version in case anyone on your mailing list wants to read it outside of their email program

A newsletter marketing program is a tremendously creative endeavour and it's rewarding for companies to see their story unfold online.

My team and I often find that new needs arise during the course of a content marketing program, and new opportunities present.

So, it's important to be flexible and respond to the changing business landscape.

But if you keep to some basic "rules of the road" your newsletter will help you develop greater brand recognition for your company, a consistent opportunity for customers and potential customers to connect with you and a the opportunity to create a stronger community of supporters for your business.

Action You Can Take Today:

Set an intention to explore the idea of a company newsletter and answer the following questions:

How often do you want to produce your newsletter?

When are you going to produce the first issue?

When are you going to meet with your team to start the ball rolling?

Who on your team are you going to make responsible for production?

Chapter Ten
Social Media Marketing

Social media has turned the world of marketing on its ear.

What's more, as it continues to evolve, I'm convinced that it will continue to create new opportunities for businesses to promote their products and services online while building a community of allies and supporters.

The implications for businesses — especially for those run by Boomers — are huge: as more members of the internet-generation filter into senior positions in the world of work, the older "tried and true" methods of doing business risk becoming increasingly irrelevant.

In fact, this is already happening: the Chief Marketing Officer (CMO) Council reports that the decisions of 85% of BtoB buyers are affected by online content (http://www.corporate-eye.com/main/85-of-b2b-buyers-say-online-content-affects-purchase-decisions/).

Furthermore, in order to compete, businesses need to become publishing houses with an eye on providing value for the customer.

But publishing content is just one part of the equation: social media is how you tell people that the content exists. The most successful businesses going forward will be the ones that can adapt to flexible ways of delivering information and doing business.

In other words, the train is now leaving the station. Businesses need to make sure they are on it. A lot of the businesses I work with feel a little suspicious of social media marketing, in the beginning, at least.

They are not the least bit interested in what celebrities eat for breakfast or where their friends from high school are now living.

But rather than look at social media as some newfangled *thang,* I invite you to see it as a tried and true method for generating business leads. What's more:

1. It can demonstrate that your company has an organized and well-established online program for keeping in touch with existing and potential customers.

2. It gives you the chance to showcase your company's products and services while highlighting the benefits of doing business with you.

3. It is a tool for developing greater rapport with your existing client base.

4. It is a tool for inviting feedback from existing and prospective clients.

5. It is a means of keeping customers connected to you…perhaps instead of, or at least in addition to, your competitors.

6. It is an opportunity to build your customer base

7. Like all other content marketing tools, a social media marketing program is an opportunity to create an online footprint for your organization that is larger than you otherwise could enjoy.

8. It's a chance for clients and prospects to get to know more about your business and give them an opportunity to like and trust you more.

9. It's an important tool for funneling people to your website where members of your sales team can have the opportunity to enjoy the types of conversations that might lead to a sale.

What Is Social Media Marketing?

Those of us in the field tend to throw the term "social media marketing" around as though it's been part of our world since the Dawn of Time but if you're new to the concept it's helpful to have a clear definition. So here's my take:

"Social media marketing is the process of starting conversations that might lead to sales through one or more social media sites."
Susan Crossman

There is a strategy to this. Your social media platforms are like officials standing along the route of a marathon and their goal is to direct the runners to their final destination. In this case, that destination is your website.

And to make the analogy really work, imagine that all of your competitors have officials standing along the same route and they are trying to direct the runners to their websites as well.

If you haven't asked any officials to stand out there and show people how to get to your website, none of those "runners" are going to find their way to it. Other people might. But not the people participating in the marathon. In this case, the people in the marathon represent everybody on the internet who might be interested in what you are selling.

Seen in that light, doesn't social media make more sense?

The conversations you're looking to start with social media could start on the social media platform itself but it's just as likely that they might start on your website.

Every social media site is different and each one attracts a different demographic. So knowing who you want to do business with is important. (See: Personas, Chapter Four)

According to the Pew Research Centre's statistics for 2014 (http://www.pewinternet.org/data-trend/social-media/social-media-user-demographics/), 75% of internet users visit social media sites and this includes:

- 89% of internet users aged 18-29
- 82% of internet users aged 30-49
- 65% of internet users aged 50-64 and
- 49% of internet users aged 65+

Of all adults aged 18+ who are active online,

- 58% use Facebook
- 23% use LinkedIn
- 22% use Pinterest and
- 21% use Instagram
- 19% use Twitter

Pew also reports that 52% of online adults now use two or more social media sites, with a particular note that Linked In usage is growing among professionals and college graduates.

As of this writing, there were 347 million people using Linked In, with two people joining the platform every second. (Source: http://expandedramblings.com/index.php/by-the-numbers-a-few-important-linkedin-stats/)

Brandon Brodzky, founder and CEO of Invision Consulting, further reports that the total number of users for each platform break down as follows:

Facebook:	1.32 billion
Linked In:	300 million
Twitter:	271 million
Instagram:	200 million
Pinterest:	70 million

Brodzky notes that there are seven billion people in the world, roughly three billion of whom are on the internet. This is a very large number of people. Is it possible that some of your customers or their influencers are among them?

(Source: https://www.linkedin.com/pulse/20141118182103-28964915-social-media-user-statistics-age-demographics-for-2014)

Social media itself is a catch-all term for sites that may provide radically different social actions.

For instance, Twitter is a social site designed to let people share short messages or "updates" with others. You can share photos and join "Tweet-ups" to connect with other people.

Facebook, by contrast, is a much more robust social networking site that allows for sharing updates, photos, joining events, creating and joining private groups, and many other activities.

The online environment is substantially more sophisticated than it was even five years ago and that is going to continue to change.

Linked In, Facebook, Twitter and You Tube are the channels that are probably best-known today, but Google +, Instagram, Pinterest, and others, are also popular.

While they are each unique, and they are each evolving in their own way, I think it's safe to say that there are a number of aspects of the social media world in general that are going to stay constant. Specifically:

- Social media is friendly, conversational, immediate and unpredictable.

- There are many different avenues for staking your business presence in social media and they almost always connect, so whether we realize it or not, we are creating an identity network that allows potential customers to see us from a variety of viewpoints and engage with us from different angles. Your business needs to have profiles on numerous platforms, if only just to claim the space; posting regularly gives the crucial added benefit of boosting your search engine rankings.

- There are many different ways to play with social media and many different expert opinions on how to do it "right." For example, Twitter may be an effective platform for some businesses. But if your clients and customers do not show up there, it's pointless to expect a lot of valuable engagement. Google and other search engines are always watching, however, and it is vital to have a strong presence on a variety of social media platforms, if only to boost your search engine rankings. *Is* there a right way and a wrong way? No! Because this world is continually evolving you need to play a little – trial and error is expected! You go with what works until it doesn't anymore.

- Knowledge of and comfort with social media grow over time. The goal is to build your online community, communicate with members of your community, lead them back to your website where they can find out more about what you offer and, hopefully, start conversations with your potential customers about how you can meet their needs. Your strategy will evolve – what feels right and comfortable in the beginning will give way to other ideas and opportunities for serving your clients and prospective clients. Be flexible!

Social Media and Search

Even if your ideal clients don't spend much time hanging out on social media sites, there are very real search engine benefits to being active on social media.

For one thing, your various social media platforms will include the opportunity to include a link back to your website, which supports search engine activity.

What's more, when people search for what you offer, it's quite possible that the search engines will pick up your social media platform information, thereby enabling you to show up more powerfully online.

And, indeed, many people perform searches on the social media sites themselves to find content that's relevant to them. If you have a presence there, you have the opportunity to show up in those searches, which will lead people to your platform profile and thence on to your website, *where you can start a conversation that might lead to a sale.*

A Word on Cost

If you've ever bought advertising space in a traditional newspaper or magazine, you know how painful it can be to part with thousands of dollars for an ad that might, or might not, get seen by your ideal customer.

Although the news outlet in whose publication you are advertising might be able to tell you it has a circulation of 100,000, that doesn't mean that every single one of those people are looking for what you're selling, and it certainly doesn't guarantee that they will ever notice the ad you've agreed to buy.

You can get a lot more exposure to your target audience online, and you can determine to a much greater degree who is seeing your ads online, than you ever could with a print magazine.

You still have to be targeted with your online advertising and marketing dollars, but the internet is set up to facilitate being found.

You will have manpower costs associated with ensuring that someone is cultivating your "social media garden," and if you decide to do some online advertising, that can cost you money as well; but if your online presence is strategically managed, your dollars are far more likely to generate results than advertising in traditional media. And this, too, can take some time.

You are also much closer to your customers and potential customers online than ever before: people can post reviews of your products and services, rate customer service and ask questions or express their concerns directly to you through your social media platforms. Which gives you the opportunity to build good relationships with your customers.

You need to be on top of all of this, however, and this is why some companies are now hiring social media community managers.

A lot of business people I talk to are nervous that they might get negative attention online or that somebody might post awful things about them through social media.

They worry that this will damage their reputation. This actually happened recently to one of my clients that has a very active social media presence. We had posted a link to our newsletter on our private group on LinkedIn and one of our readers took exception to some of the information that had been included in the article. This man posted a comment that publicly stated he thought the article was inaccurate and misleading and that we should check our facts before publishing.

My client is an industry leader with an international presence and we have thousands of people, all of them potential clients, in that group. The information in question had come from a respected industry expert but the article was phrased in a way that could be seen as ambiguous and it was possibly open to some misinterpretation.

My client was understandably worried about the claim that we were misleading people and we posted a response to the comment that:

- Thanked the reader for their vigilance and their concern
- Told the reader that we valued their input
- Reminded readers generally that we strive for accuracy and
- Asked the reader if we could email him directly to discuss the issue in more detail.

The reader was glad to be acknowledged and he had made some good points.

We revised the article to take his points into consideration and because he himself was an expert in this area, we asked him to review the revised article to ensure we had our facts straight.

Then we took the revised article back to the person from whom we had originally received the information, and asked her to review the man's changes.

Once we had a revision everybody was happy with, we posted a new link to it in the LinkedIn group, along with our thanks to the reader for helping us maintain the credibility and value of the information we share.

Case closed. Everybody was happy.

Now, it does happen that sometimes you get a comment from someone who is substantially less interested in quality information than they are about the need to bring someone, anyone, to their knees online. You can't do much about those people. If they try to post a comment to your blog, you don't have to publish it if your blog is located on your website. So no one sees it.

But social media is the Wild West and if someone makes a nasty comment on social media, your best bet is to maintain a reasoned and reasonable response, and politely steer the conversation offline.

If they just won't go, your calm, cool, and collected responses will demonstrate to other readers that the guy is out of line and they will usually come to the defense of you, the wronged party.

But it's been my experience that those attacks rarely happen.

The benefits of social media far outweigh the disadvantages and if we spend our entire lives in fear of what other people are going to say about us we will never benefit from the good things that social media can deliver.

So how do you maximize your social media presence? Here are a few pointers for each of the main platforms.

Linked In

Why use LinkedIn:
- LinkedIn is an 11-year-old business-focused social networking site that aims to help people network professionally. More than 300 million business professionals use LinkedIn (100 million users in the US and 9 million in Canada) and chances are good that the people you want to do business with, the decision makers at least, are there.

- 40% of users check LinkedIn daily, 18% spend more than 7 hours per week on the platform

- If you aren't active on LinkedIn it's possible that your competition is – why give them the advantage?

- A robust LinkedIn profile demonstrates to potential customers and potential employers that you are engaged as a member of a community – a network of professionals. It lends credibility to you and to your organization and it helps support search engine rankings for your company.

What LinkedIn is:

LinkedIn is a way to communicate with the people you would like to do business with and it permits you to cultivate relationships with them in a way you might not otherwise be able to do.

It allows you to build a community by connecting with business associates, clients, and colleagues who you already know.

Once you have "connected" with them, they then become part of your own personal network and you can send them inmail messages. They can also see what you're posting in your news stream.

Once you've connected with a person, you will then have access to their list of connections – this is called your "extended network" — and you can request an introduction to people in your extended network through your mutual contacts.

LinkedIn also provides other features, including the ability to set up and join groups, and it has a jobs section where members can advertise open positions or apply for jobs.

The basic service is free and it is very, very powerful, both as a method of connecting and as a means of establishing your credibility.

How do you use LinkedIn as a lead generation tool?

1. **Maximize your profile.** Make sure you have a friendly, but professional, photo on your profile and that you fill in all fields, i.e. previous work experience, education, skills and capabilities

2. **Connect with the people you have met,** for example at a conference or a business networking event, and send them a short note within the connection invitation itself. I often will say a few brief words about how I can assist them and invite them to contact me if they feel I can be of assistance.

3. **Send people inmails.** When someone connects with you, if they are in your target market, send them a nice note asking if they would like to schedule a conversation about how you can help them meet their goals – perhaps you can help them save money, develop efficiencies or enrich an experience.

4. **Leverage your brand:** establish and join a group page for your company, and comment on and like information that is posted there.

5. **Comment on people's updates.** As your prospects' information shows up in your news stream, comment on it, like it and send them a message about it.

6. **Find out what groups your prospects belong to and join them,** then monitor them for opportunities to comment. When someone makes a comment you like, or you see an area where your company can help them,

you can answer them in the group or direct message them – you can't inmail anyone you aren't connected to unless you upgrade from the free Linked In account but you CAN message anyone who is a part of any group you belong to. You can join up to 500 groups.

7. **Connect with prospects you locate in your group monitoring activities** – you don't need the email addresses of anyone who belongs to the same group to which you belong. By contrast, you cannot connect with someone whose email address you do not already have.

8. **Ask for introductions** to the people with whom you would like to start a sales-oriented conversation.

9. **Ask people you know well to give you recommendations.**

Implications of all of this activity:

The goal of being active on LinkedIn is to cultivate relationships with people you might not otherwise get to meet. So, for example, if your prospects don't turn up at the networking events or conferences you attend, you might be able to find a way to "meet" them on LinkedIn.

LinkedIn works best when you have a strategy, and when you consistently work at maximizing the opportunity.

Facebook

Why use Facebook:

- Statistics for Facebook change by the moment but as of this writing it is one of the most popular social media sites, acting as a kind of "home base" for people who are active online.

- More than 1.1 billion people are registered users of Facebook

- 700 million people are on the platform every day, staying for an average of 20 minutes per visit

- There are more than 2 billion connections between local businesses and people on the site

- 70% of users are connected to and engage with a local business (US statistic)

- 47% of Americans say that FB has a larger impact on their purchasing behaviour than any other SM network

- 67% of B to C marketers have generated leads using FB

(Source: Hubspot http://www.hubspot.com/marketing-statistics-1)

Again, with so many people using Facebook it stands to reason that some of those people could be members of your target audience or their influencers.

Although you might not be maximizing the opportunity to promote your business on Facebook, your competitors could well be doing so. Why leave the field to someone else entirely?

I run into a lot of people who feel resistant to either having a presence on Facebook or being active on that platform.

At its heart, Facebook is simply a social networking site that allows people to connect with other people they know and share their news.

I remember my oldest daughter trying to explain the concept of Facebook to me some years ago when she was away at university.

She told me that she had this wall and people were posting on it. She could tell people about a party she was hosting and people could respond on the wall.

To a woman whose university computer experience involved going to a special room where you punched holes in cards, this was way beyond my ken. Where was the wall, I wanted to know.

"Well it's not a real wall," she said. "It's just on the internet."

Huh?

I can't wait to find out what crazy ideas her children are going to use to befuddle *her*.

What Faacebook is:

Facebook is a social media networking site that allows you to build a community while communicating with people who might want to do business with you – or their influencers.

Facebook was, in fact, invented originally for college students. Since its creation in 2004 it has grown explosively to become the world's largest social network with more than 1-billion users worldwide.

Now, presumably as a business you are not hoping to invite people to a lot of parties, (although, on the other hand, that might be a good idea, too!).

But you do want to invite people to do business with you and in order to do that you need to start conversations with them that might lead to a sale.

How Do You Do That?

1. **Set up a Facebook Page for Your Business.** It's actually quite easy to establish a FB page and the platform at this point in time makes it a relatively straightforward process. There are instructions to walk you through the steps reasonably carefully. You want to select images for your page that are consistent with the images you use on your other branding materials – your logo, for example — and your business description should be the standard one you use elsewhere that explains what you do for whom, and how you do it.

2. **Start Posting on Your Page Consistently.** Relevant topics might include:

   - News of any educational webinars you're running (with a link back to your website where the main information is posted)

   - Attendance at any upcoming conferences (with an invitation to people to link back to your website for more information)

   - Any speaking engagements your executive might be undertaking

   - Interesting articles you've found online that are helpful to your customers – perhaps on industry-related or government websites

   - Links to articles on your website that relate to customer issues

- Links to your regular blog postings
- Links to your You Tube videos
- Images of interest to your customers
- Notice of promotions and hires within your company
- Links to your online newsletter
- Images of your products, people and promotions
- Pictures from the company barbecue, bowling or fundraising events

3. **Invite people to "Like" your page.** Use your other social media channels and your website to invite people to "Like" you on Facebook. They need to have their own Facebook page in order to do this but once they "Like" you, your news will show up in their newstream. The more creative and inventive your posts are, the better your opportunities will be to encourage people to do business with you. And, of course, you want to "Like" the Facebook pages of your customers.

4. **Invite Engagement.** With Facebook, you can ask your customers to share news of how you've helped them solve a problem or recognize great service people or sales reps. You can ask customers questions and use their responses in an upcoming blog post or case study. You can also solicit details about innovative uses of your product or "good news" information that might be relevant for media coverage.

5. **Think Outside the Box.** Or the platform, as the case may be. Facebook has all kinds of applications that allow you to invite people to sign up for your company newsletter, for example, or shop online. There are applications that let you get customer support through Facebook or download coupons. You can run contests on Facebook, giving people the opportunity to win prizes in exchange for their best product-related stories, or for winning a draw that requires them to provide their email addresses (thus growing your database as well).

Implications of all of this activity:

Facebook is a great way to keep your company name in front of your customers and prospects, provided you post consistently and ensure the content you are posting is interesting, lively, informative and relevant.

Facebook can increase brand awareness, improve engagement, increase traffic to your website and ultimately contribute to more business.

It also gives your business another opportunity to rank with the search engines, so it increases your online findability as well.

Twitter

Why Use Twitter:
- Twitter is popular and accessible and, as a social media tool, it lets you establish a branded Twitter feed and continuously share (140-character) news briefs about your business

- It puts your business name in front of customers and prospective customers

- About 36% of Twitter users visit the site daily (Source: Hubspot http://www.hubspot.com/marketing-statistics-1)

- Your can use your tweets on Twitter to link to your website, Facebook profile, YouTube channel or other online property where people can obtain information about your company

- You can add a hashtag to your tweet (such as #superiorservice or #manufacturing) to expand your reach beyond the people who are following you and allow people who might be searching for the hashtag topic to find your tweet about it

- Because Twitter is such an immediate platform, you can quickly address the needs of your customers where necessary or desirable

What it is:
Twitter is an online platform that allows you to build a community where you can invite engagement, share news about your company, develop thought leadership and promote your brand. It allows you to gain access to people with whom you might not ordinarily connect and communicate with them in comments using a maximum of 140 characters.

How Do You Do That?

1. Be clear on who your ideal customers are (see the information about "Personas" in Chapter 4).

2. Set up your Twitter profile, making sure all information, including any images you use, are consistent with your brand.

3. Start following your customers, as well as your potential and prospective customers

4. Start tweeting. Generally speaking you want about 70% of your tweets to be about topics that don't promote your own company. This might include links to online articles of interest in your industry, observations about the field in which you operate, internal company news, support for charities you support, calls for new hires, etc.

5. Use the other 30% of your tweets to direct people to your website, Facebook, Linked In or You Tube channels, where they will find more information about your company, special offers, registration pages for your newsletter, upcoming webinar or other promotional event, etc.

6. Respond quickly to any tweets that request service, air a complaint or express concern about your business.

7. Acknowledge shout-outs and compliments.

8. Retweet (RT) people to show them a little "Twitter Love."

9. Direct Message people where appropriate. You can't DM someone who doesn't follow you but the standard etiquette is that if someone follows you, you follow

them back. Not everybody has this policy but that is one way to generate more follows on the platform. Don't auto-DM people – it's boorish.

10. Include photos in your tweets

11. Don't spam people.

Implications of all of this activity:
Twitter is another great way to keep your company name in front of your customers and prospects, provided they use the platform. The business applications of Twitter are still evolving and access is still an issue: the people who are managing the Twitter feed of many businesses tend to be junior community managers, rather than the decision makers, so if you are a BtoB company, your chances of speaking directly to the decision-makers are not great.

That being said, an active Twitter presence gives you another way to show up in the search engines, and another way for people to search for you, find you, and get an impression of your business and your brand.

Even if you are not holding out high hopes for generating business in this fashion, you still need to be there because you just never know. I've had business leads from Twitter and I've made good connections on this platform that have helped me develop my business. You need to be there.

Google+

Why Use Google +:
- Google+ is a relative newcomer to the social media game (2011) but the number of people using it is growing and, since this IS a Google product, there is

no end in sight. As of January, 2015, there were 2.2 billion people using Google+, although Business Insider Magazine reported that just a little less than 10% of users are active on the platform. (Source: http://www.businessinsider.com/google-active-users-2015-1). This is bound to grow substantially over the next couple of years so it's probably a good idea to add it to your online "playlist."

- Google gets more than 67% of the internet's search engine volume (Source: http://searchengineland.com/google-search-share-stable-bing-continues-cannibalize-yahoo-187124) , which means Google+ posts carry more weight (from a link equity perspective) as a result

- The Google+ Circles allow you to share some information with people in one group but not others, allowing you to differentiate between posts directed to your friends and family, and posts directed to your business connections

- Google+ Hangouts allow users to gather in video meetings that you can also record and post to YouTube.

- The platform enables you to invite contacts to an event and notify them directly; their RSVP automatically triggers a calendar addition for them, all of which expands the potential impact of your invitation.

What Google+ Is:

Google+ is a social platform stemming from your Google Account that allows you to easily build a community, invite engagement, share news about your company, develop thought leadership and promote your brand.

It provides another opportunity to gain access to people with whom you might not ordinarily connect and communicate with them.

You add contacts to "circles" that represent your areas of interest and to which you can post specific, circle-oriented content.

How Do You Do That?

Engagement on Google+ is similar to Twitter and Facebook. But in general you engage through:

Image sharing
Images have an important role in the Google+ community so make sure you make generous use of appropriate images in your posting.

Connecting with Influencers
You want to look for and connect with clients and customers, prospective clients and customers, business contacts, and, most particularly, influencers. Don't spam anybody, of course and make sure your content is professional and appropriate to the circle to which you are posting.

Creating Good Content
You want to give people a reason to get excited about your business and your brand so consistently developing good content is important. As mentioned, you can determine who gets to see which content you post, which allows you to be creative and expressive in your postings.

Engaging
As with any social media platform, it isn't just about broadcasting your message. The idea is to start the conversations that might lead to a sale and you're doing that by building a community of people who know they need what

you offer. To take full advantage of the opportunity, you need to engage them – "like" (+1) their content, comment on it and be available to converse.

Responding
If a follower asks a question or comes to you for help with an issue, answer their questions and respond to their inquiry.

Frequency and Scheduling
You can schedule your posts with a platform such as Hootsuite (see Chapter 15 -- "Tools") so play with timing a little to see what time of day is best to post. This may change over time so be sensitive to changes.

Avoiding Spam
As with all social networks, don't annoy people with endless announcements of upcoming events. The idea is engagement, not continuous self-promotion, and you will irritate the very people with whom you would like to do business if all you're doing is promoting yourself.

Using +Name
You can give your Google+ contacts a shout-out and link directly to their Google+ page by typing a "+" and then typing their name. This will trigger a notification to them to tell them that you're talking about them. Google+ facilitates the process with a drop-down. This is important when you're including an author name for a post you want to share, for example.

Implications of all of this activity:
Although it's a relative newcomer to the social media game, it's likely that Google+ is destined for greatness.

As a Google property, it connects to all of the major Google channels that we've come to depend on, such as Google Search, Google Drive, Gmail, Analytics, Adwords, Calendar, You Tube, and plenty more. And many people feel that activity on Google+ is likely to boost your search engine results as a result of its connection to Google.

Provided your customers are on Google+, you have a prime opportunity to keep your company name in front of them.

And although the business applications of G+ are still evolving, a presence there is likely to at the very least boost your search engine results and give your potential customers another opportunity to find you, and get an impression of your business and your brand.

YouTube

Why Use YouTube?

- Many B2B marketers rank YouTube as the second most effective social network (after LinkedIn) (http://blog.marketingv2.com/5-ways-manufacturing-companies-can-use-social-media-marketing)

Video can increase click-through rates by upwards of 96%. (http://www.prnewswire.com/news-releases/getresponse-study-shows-video-emails-increase-click-through-rates-by-96-percent-78406237.html)

- /blog/25-amazing-video-marketing-statistics/)

- Because analytics let you see which videos each lead watched, and for how long, you can segment, score and nurture leads based on the data gathered

- People spend 80% more time on video blogs than regular blogs, and they remember a video more than a month after having watched it (http://blog.hubspot.com/blog/tabid/6307/bid/33423/19

-Reasons-You-Should-Include-Visual-Content-in-Your-Marketing-Data.aspx)

If your customers, or their influencers, are likely watching videos on YouTube that are related to your industry, then you should have a YouTube channel.

- YouTube gets more than 1 billion unique visits every month

- Other Other social media platforms, such as Google+, Facebook, and Twitter, are integrated with YouTube: users can watch videos directly from their feeds.

- Good content on YouTube allows viewers to get to know your brand better and see your business in a positive light.

- YouTube visitors watch around six billion hours of video every month

(https://www.youtube.com/yt/press/statistics.html)

What YouTube Is

YouTube is a free video-sharing platform that acts as a distribution platform for people and businesses.

The latest statistics assert that more than one billion people from around the world use the platform, and hundreds of hours of video are uploaded every minute.
(Source: https://www.youtube.com/yt/press/statistics.html)

The potential audience on YouTube, therefore, is massive – far larger than what you can expect to see on your own website —

and YouTube video content ranks higher than other content in search engine results.

Having a presence on YouTube also allows you to expand your appeal to people who, simply put, don't like to read.

You can embed your videos onto your website and stream them from YouTube (which saves hosting space on your site).

How Do You Use It?

Your YouTube videos can be everything from a company overview that gives people a strong sense of what your company does and how you do it, to instructional videos aimed at showing potential customers how your product or service works.

Some of your videos, therefore, should be focused on expressing your company's brand promise, while others might better be focused on converting viewers to buyers. Ideally this takes a strategy. And, at this point in time, a relatively large budget.

Yes, YouTube is accessible to anyone with an iPhone and the technical skills that allow you to edit and post your video to YouTube. But in a perfect world, you want your videos to be professionally produced and edited. It's worth the investment.

This is your brand we're talking about, and we live in a world where people have been conditioned by Hollywood, network television and big brand name companies to expect stunning videos with high production values.

In fact, one of my colleagues runs a video content marketing production company and he is constantly frustrated by the fact that most people do not understand how far the dollar will actually go in the video world. Clients will send him links to marketing videos they've found online that they like. They want their $15,000 company video to be just like it. But the one they like was quite possibly a $100,000 video that used numerous locations, plenty of different cameras, studio work and sophisticated graphic treatment.

Yes you can do it with an iPhone and yes there are stock video companies out there now where you can find snippets to add in to your video. But you still want someone who knows what they're doing with equipment that will reflect well on your brand to manage your video production program.

Any videos you produce for your company might fall into a number of categories, including:

Thought leadership
Videos that show you or another company representative speaking intelligently about issues that are important in your industry.

This might include content of a more academic nature (speeches, seminar material) or tips about a specific area relevant to your company.

Tutorials and How-to's
You can get instructions on doing almost anything on YouTube and almost any business can create a video that demonstrates some aspect of how to do something that falls within its area of expertise.

Advertisements
There is certainly the opportunity for paid advertising on YouTube and although paid ads don't help with content ranking, they can add authority to your channel.

Brand Support
A company overview or a short history of the company might fall into this category.

Video News Releases

Video news releases (VNR's) add extra shine to your news and can increase your chances of media pickup.

Implications of all of this activity:

You Tube is a fabulous way to generate brand recognition, thought leadership, leads and search engine attention.

A presence on this platform gives you another way to show up in the search engines, and another way for people to search for you, find you, and get an impression of your business and your brand. YouTube is a powerful platform and, if you nurture your presence there with professional videos, it can be a great option for developing business opportunity.

Action You Can Take Today:

Do a Social Media Audit of Your Business. Using the following chart on the next page:

On a scale of 1-10, with 10 meaning "We're Rocking It!" rank your company's social media presence according to the following criteria:

And be sure to connect with me and my team on our social media platforms: Connect with me, Susan Crossman on LinkedIn; Follow me on Twitter (@CrossmanCom)
Like the Crossman Communications Facebook page
Add Susan Crossman and Crossman Communications to your circles on Google+ and/or
If you'd like to know more about how Crossman Communications can support your content marketing objectives, contact me directly at susan@crossmancommunications.com

Criteria	Score Out of 10				
	Linked In	Facebook	Twitter	Google+	YouTube
Visual appeal					
Corporate branding, i.e. How well have you portrayed brand?					
How well have you maintained a 40-60 split between broadcasting your own news and sharing other information?					
How well do you provide the benefits of your product or service rather than just the features of them?					
How well do you include "Calls to Action"					
Do all of your links work?					

Chapter Eleven
Email Database Marketing

A lot of small business owners are reluctant to get involved with email marketing because:

a) They feel they themselves are already getting too many emails (why would they want to bring more into the world?) and

b) They aren't sure how the process works

But email marketing can be a highly effective way of positioning your company's products and services with customers and potential customers.

This isn't something that you just tackle on an ad hoc basis.

Ideally, you develop a well-planned email marketing strategy that involves multiple campaigns scheduled according to a specific calendar.

Ideally, you schedule your email campaigns to minimize the likelihood that you are going to overwhelm or annoy customers and prospects.

And, if you are providing information that may be of value to people, in a consistent, and non-intrusive manner, you will be able to achieve your goals and develop more leads.

Easier said than done, right?

We will often recommend an email marketing program because:

1. It demonstrates that your company has an organized and well-established program for keeping in touch with customers

2. It gives you the chance to showcase your company's products and the benefits of doing business with you.

3. It can be a tool for developing greater rapport with your existing client base.

4. It can be a tool for inviting feedback from existing and prospective clients.

5. It is a means of keeping customers and potential customers connected to you…perhaps instead of (or at least in addition to), your competitors.

6. Like all other content marketing tools, an email marketing program is an opportunity to create a footprint for your organization that is larger than you otherwise could enjoy

7. It's a chance for clients and prospects to get to know more about your business and give them an opportunity to know, like and trust you more.

8. It is an important tool for funneling people to members of your sales team where they can have the types of conversations that might lead to a sale.

In addition, email marketing is much less expensive than many other forms of communication and it can generate good leads. It allows you to target your ideal customers with relative ease and the return on investment can be excellent — without the need for killing a single tree!

Not only that, but analytics make it easy to measure how successful your email campaigns are. A consistent email marketing program allows you to generate greater brand awareness and the positive regard of your email recipients.

What is Email Marketing?

Generally speaking, email marketing is the process of directly marketing a business offer to a group of people via their email addresses.

You can probably understand why it generates a lot of emotional discussion in the marketing field, and why the Canadian government has introduced legislation to limit how we go about the business of emailing people whose business we desire.

(See http://fightspam.gc.ca/eic/site/030.nsf/eng/home for more information about the legislation). Some people do abuse the process.

We all get a ton of email already and, as in the days before the Internet, nobody actually wants to see a stream of junk mail flooding out of their mailbox and into their life.

Remember the days when we had to sort through stacks of paper flyers in order to get to the actual letters, bills and magazines in our mailbox? Well, that's still happening in the real world to some extent.

And the issue has made the leap to email. The Canadian government wants to limit how that works in the virtual world.

Its regulations relate to how you build the list of email addresses you use for emailing, and we'll get to that in a moment. For now, let's look a little deeper at what email marketing is, and how it might help your business develop more leads.

While every email you send to an existing or potential customer might be considered email marketing, we tend to think of "Email Marketing" as a specific process that involves the list of email addresses you've collected in order to stay in touch with your customer base.

The emails you're sending out might be promotional in nature (i.e. they tell people about a seasonal sale, special discount, short-term offer or other sales-oriented opportunity), or they might be designed to encourage customer loyalty and position your business more effectively in the marketplace.

If you manufacture gardening equipment, for example, and you're bringing out a new model of weed whipper in time for next spring, you might send a promotional email out to your distributors this June offering a 15% discount on the current year's models.

You might also decide to publish a regular newsletter to share information about your company, your products and your services, so that customers and prospects can learn more about you and "warm up" to the idea of doing business with you.

This kind of "retention email" serves to increase brand recognition and help you stay connected with your clients while promoting your business at the same time.

You might also decide to send a "welcome" email to anyone who opts in to your list. Welcome letters can not only provide valuable information about your company, they can also serve as a vehicle for asking your new contacts for key information about the particular products or services they're looking for. This can help you add them to a specific list that will let you fine tune your offer to them in future.

Other email campaign opportunities include sending out announcements on products or services, a newsletter regarding your company and/or or coupons for future purchases.

One of our clients uses email specifically to help leverage their conference and tradeshow participation. They are very well respected in their industry and they participate in and sponsor many trade shows throughout North America.

As an exhibitor, they will often receive, free of charge, a list of the people who have registered to attend an upcoming show. Sometimes these lists must be purchased from conference organizers and the going rate at this point is about $400-$500.

This is a highly qualified list, of course, but the purchase cost is intended to be limited to two, sometimes a maximum of three, email mailings only.

For a two-mailing list, we will send one mailing a few days before the show begins to invite participants to our client's booth and give them an idea of what they will find there (a draw for an iPad, iWatch, barbecue , etc.).

The second mailing we will send out after the show with an invitation to sign up to receive the company's newsletter. Another option would be to offer the opportunity to download a White Paper, "Tip List" or other Irresistible Free Offer (IFO).

Ultimately, we want to migrate them onto our existing database list so that we can continue to communicate with them so that we can, wait for it, *start conversations with them that might lead to a sale*.

One of the advantages of email marketing is that the delivery systems we use to facilitate sending the emails allow us to track how many people received the email, how many people opened it, and how many people took action by clicking on a link that we included in the content. We can thus track our return on investment and determine what types of email content get us the best response. It's real "trial and error" stuff.

And it all happens without buying a stamp or stuffing a single envelope.

Since most people are in their inbox at least once a day, email marketing allows you to deliver your message to a location where your customers are going to be spending time anyway.

The trick is to ensure they open the email and see what you're offering.

Email servers have become increasingly sophisticated in their ability to filter out email messages that might be considered "spammy," and this does limit how many emails are actually getting in front of your target audience.

And that's why the concept of "opting in" has become so relevant: the more people who take action to ask to receive your emails, the more likely you are to get your message in front of them.

My team and I generally use a mail delivery service called "MailChimp" for client email campaigns.

There is a free version of the platform available as an introductory service, but as you increase the number of people in your list, you need to move along to the paid service. Fees are scaled according to the size of your database.

MailChimp has more than eight-million users who send billions of emails every month, and the company tracks their data so they know what "average" response rates are in a long list of industry sectors.

MailChimp notes that their customers range from one-person startups to Fortune 500 companies, and they share their information so you can see how your company relates to the benchmark set by others in your industry.

If you would like to see their statistics from early spring, 2015, please visit:

http://mailchimp.com/resources/research/email-marketing-benchmarks/.

Becoming familiar with your own email analytics will help you improve your email marketing efforts for better results.

So what do the terms mean?

Open rate reflects the number of people who saw the email land in their inbox and actually opened it to read it.

If your open rate is below the benchmark for your industry, then you probably need to improve the subject lines you're using.

We have some concerns that a company's virus scanners can send back false open rate statistics but the field is divided as to how much of a problem this is and which email service providers are most at risk.

The business of spam filters is also an issue and it, also, is extremely complex.

It's easy to get lost in the detail of how scanning and filtering work and to be honest there is no guarantee that your email will be opened by the people you want to reach, or that most of the recipients will open your emails.

Email marketing is a long-term play and results take a long time to really start to show up.

Suffice to say that if you are getting unsubscribes and clicks on your emails, then you are getting opens.

Click rate refers to the number of people who take action on the links you provide in your email.

Ideally you want to send people to a landing page on your web page where they will have the opportunity to deepen their connection with you. This might be by signing up for a free webinar or downloading your Easy Guide to Saving Money with your products and services.

If your click rate is low, then you either don't have high numbers of your target audience members on your database or you need to give people more compelling reasons to click through to your website.

Hard bounces in your email results means that you have email addresses that need to be deleted – i.e. there is a problem with the email address or server associated with a hard bounce and it's never going to be fixed.

Soft bounces mean there is a temporary problem with the email address or its delivery, and it might be fixed in time for the next send.

You want your **abuse rate** to be very, very low – that number represents how many people have complained about the emails you are sending them and, if that rate is high, it indicates you are possibly using unprofessional methods for growing your list. You could get locked out of your email service as a result.

Unsubscribes are a normal part of email marketing – people opt in to your list and they opt out.

If you are sending quality emails to people who want to receive them, your chances of keeping your unsubscribe rate low (and, by extension, your abuse rate) are pretty good.

Does company size matter when it comes to your email marketing statistics? Let's see what MailChimp has to say about it:

Average Email Campaign Stats of MailChimp Customers by Company Size:

Company Size	Open Rate	Click Rate	Soft Rate	Hard Rate	Abuse Rate	Unsub Rate
1 to 10	22.15%	3.12%	0.75%	0.59%	0.04%	0.30%
11 to 25	21.22%	2.78%	0.70%	0.55%	0.03%	0.25%
26-50	22.16%	3.16%	0.47%	0.36%	0.02%	0.18%
50+	23.57%	3.06%	0.70%	0.63%	0.03%	0.21%

Email marketing takes some trial and error and a fair bit of organization is required in order to make it work. It's a good idea to have an editorial calendar in place so you can set out a production schedule with deadlines that will allow you to maximize your promotional opportunities for the entire year. And database management is an important part of the process as well.

Here are some other tips for maximizing your success rate with email marketing:

- Use straightforward subject lines that simply state what recipients can expect to find inside the email.

- Make sure your company name appears in the "From" and subject line fields of the email so that people will know right away who is sending it – people are less likely to complain of abuse if they recognize the sender's name.

- Use undramatic language in your email overall and avoid ALL CAPS, dollar signs, and excessive use of exclamation marks — these can trigger spam filters to close the door on your email.

- Make sure your email messaging is consistent with what you're using in your other marketing efforts.

- Include links back to your website, in particular to pages where recipients have a chance to take action – order a free download, purchase something, watch a promotional video, etc.

- Test to see which days of the week and times of day net you a better response rate. Do you tend to get a higher open rate when you schedule the email for Tuesdays at 9:00 a.m. or Friday afternoons at noon a better bet?

- People's email addresses change, and you can expect that there will be some bounces every time you send a mass email. Keeping in touch regularly gives people a chance to manage their subscription preferences and update their email addresses with you, if they want to keep receiving your emails.

A Word About Permission

This is a fairly intense topic and I've seen a lot of discussion online about it. And I've seen a lot of abuse.

No matter what country you call home, and what the laws on the topic there are, you are best served by making sure you have people's permission to send them email.

If you don't have this permission, they might mark your message as "spam"— which translates roughly as unsolicited commercial email. If that happens, your email accounts could be closed and your website suspended. In Canada, you are also breaking a federal law, the penalty for which could be financially crippling.

What's more, sales works best when there is a relationship involved between the buyer and the seller and that relationship requires a high degree of trust.

Do you trust people who do things (like draft you onto their email list) behind your back?

In Canada our laws require a double opt-in process, which means people have to tick a box that says "add me to your email list" and, when they receive an email from you to confirm that they want to be on your email list, they have to click on the appropriate link in that email. And you have to be able to prove that they themselves opted in to your list.

Email marketing is a great way to generate greater brand recognition for your company and it gives your customers and potential customers a consistent opportunity to connect with you.

It takes time, energy, organization and a little trial and error for you to get the maximum benefits from an email marketing program.

But the upside can be well worth the effort.

Action You Can Take Today:

Time to Brainstorm!

Create a list of 10 emails your business could be sending out over the next year to stay in touch with your customer database.

Chapter Twelve
Online PR

A public relations program can be an excellent way of positioning your company in the marketplace as *"the"* choice for your ideal customers.

It gives you the opportunity to tell your story your way and, if your press materials are well written and consistent in their messaging, you have an opportunity to contribute in a very powerful way to the conversation about your industry. This is a particularly useful tool now that there are so many online publications and industry organizations providing a ready outlet for news content.

Years ago, when I first wandered into the PR/marketing matrix, I and my colleagues in the PR field focused on creating press releases and sending them to the media outlets that we thought were most likely to be interested in the news we were sharing.

I can remember one day early on in my career standing at a fax machine (remember those?) feeling miffed about the fact that I was in charge of hand-feeding hundreds of personally addressed fax address sheets and an accompanying press release into the machine. It took hours.

Feeding the fax machine was not glamorous. And it didn't match my vision of what a thrilling career in PR should be like. But that was all part of it.

Now we have email. Thank goodness.

Once I had sent the press releases to our media contacts it was also my job to follow up with a phone call. That part hasn't changed – if you are serious about getting coverage for the story you are promoting, it's a good idea to call the reporter(s) or news representative whose attention you seek. *If* you can get their number. News people are busy and there are days when it seems like the whole world wants their attention.

They have a tough enough time getting the research done for the assignments they want or need to cover in a day, and they are not sitting there waiting for your news to show up... unless you are famous or have a lead on a story that is going to make them famous.

Here's how that conversation might go:

"Hi I'm calling from ABC Company. I sent you a press release this morning and I'm just calling to make sure that you received it?"

(Reporter responds. Likely they will say no they did not receive your press release so you are going to have to tell them what was in the press release.)

"Is this something you might be interested in running?"

(A yes or no answer will be forthcoming.)

"Do you need more information?"

(Reporter responds.)

Along the way you will either have the opportunity to re-send the email containing the press release or you will be brushed off with varying degrees of polite communication. Don't pester these people and don't be rude. Don't take anything they say personally. And next time you have something that might interest them, try again. But don't waste their time with "news" that they feel their readers won't find interesting.

If you do your job well, or you just get plain lucky, your business will be mentioned in the publication the next day or any one of a number of days thereafter.

Following up on press releases is time consuming work and a lot of factors influence your success. Key among them is the question of whether or not the information you are offering is actually of relevance to the publication's audience.

Although the technology has changed quite dramatically since my reluctant days at the fax machine, the process is still pretty much the same and publishers want what's valuable to their audience. Don't spam people!

Ideally, a PR program should support the other content marketing initiatives your company is undertaking and the messaging should be consistent, of course, across all platforms.

I often recommend a PR program for clients because:

1. It demonstrates that your company is a serious enough player in the market to be investing in a PR program.
2. It demonstrates that you are newsworthy.
3. It gives you an opportunity to develop a presence that is larger than the size of your company might suggest.
4. It gives you the chance to showcase your company's products and the benefits of doing business with you.

5. It is a tool for creating greater online excitement about your company.

6. It's a chance for clients and prospects to get to know more about your business and give them an opportunity to like and trust you more.

7. It is an important tool for funneling people to members of your sales team where they can have the types of conversations that might lead to a sale.

8. News stories about an organization are commonly valued at about three times the price of paid advertisements of comparable size, so it's a very cost-effective method of getting your message out.

9. The results of your online PR efforts are searchable -- every time the company name shows up in an article, it becomes one more online entry that someone can find when they search for you.

10. It is a powerful way to drive Google search rankings. An article that links back to your site signals to the web crawlers that you are a noteworthy organization.

Online technologies have revolutionized the world of PR and it's stunning how much more opportunity is out there for businesses that invest in this method of marketing.

OK Let's Go Big Picture Here: What is Online PR?

Public relations is the practice of earning online exposure for your organization in any one of the countless online publications or platforms that serve the same audience as you do. Unlike advertising, you don't pay the outlet to place your post or press release — if they feel your content is relevant to their audience, they will pick it up and post it, free of charge.

Your cost, therefore, is limited to whatever it costs to produce and distribute the content to outlets that are likely to want to run it. No ad placement fees, in other words.

The goal of PR is often to tell members of the public, prospective customers, investors, partners, employees, and other stakeholders about your organization or its activities or mission, and, often, to persuade them to develop a specific point of view about what you are offering or doing.

Keeping your organization's name in the public eye is a key goal of PR, as is cultivating a positive reputation for the organization, its management or its products. We're talking about supporting the brand, here.

We're also talking about generating better results for other aspects of your business's online communications efforts, particularly in the areas of social media and search engine optimization (SEO).

If you get this PR piece figured out, you'll see content you created (or a reasonable facsimile thereof) in an online news outlet or blog, with pick-up in any one of a number of social media platforms.

Online PR might still be supplemented with traditional PR, where you seek publication in actual newspapers, TV or radio shows and magazines.

But the focus is on the internet platforms where your customers are most likely to show up.

Now, thanks to the magic of the internet, my company and others like it can get our clients millions of what are called "impressions" with a single press release. Would that be beneficial to your company? I'm guessing yes!

Your online PR aims to attract:

- Directories, associations and organizations
- Columnists and writers
- Bloggers
- Social media users (Facebook, Google Plus, Pinterest, etc.)
- Websites & brand sites
- Web searchers
- And others of value or relevance in your industry

PR has three potential audiences: your internal audience (including your managers and employees), your external audience (including news and online outlets) and your government audience (which you are trying to influence in the area of policy).

Coming from a news background myself, I know that many journalists hold a somewhat cynical view of PR professionals, who often appear to be trying to pass unimportant material off as "news."

If your goal is to get your organization's name in print, then you need to stay focused on the information that is of value to your target outlets' audience members. Period. The delivery vehicle in PR generally might be any one of a number of initiatives, such as a:

- communication campaign
- press conference
- press release (print or video)
- feature article

- media-related interview for company spokespeople
- <u>speech</u> for a company leader to deliver at a meeting or event
- website or <u>some social media</u> content
- live or virtual event

A Word about Relationships

Relationships are key to good PR and after someone has been working successfully in the field for a while they tend to develop some good positive relationships with the people whose attention they seek on behalf of their client or employer.

It all comes down to reputation: if you are consistently focused on providing value to an outlet's audiences, and you don't stray into the danger zone of trying to pass company fluff off as news, then you will be rewarded by a willingness to publish the information you provide.

Remember way back in Chapter 4 when we talked about the importance of knowing your audience? That's still very relevant for online PR, only in this case you want to know about your audience and what's important to them in order to select where you want your message to show up AND you want to know a little bit about your target publication's audience and what's important to them.

Get a reputation for trying to get free ink for irrelevant material, and you will be consistently written off as a time-waster.

What about Social Media?

It took a while for PR practitioners to glom on to the opportunities presented by social media. Fifteen years ago, social media was an emerging concept and change is often hard to implement in established fields run by older people.

Let's face it, in the early years of this century, most of the senior jobs in PR would have been held by people in their 40's who were no more interested in tweeting than flying to the moon. Facebook? Kidstuff! LinkedIn? Why? No, thank you, social media was not a serious way to garner positive attention for one's clients and stakeholders.

And, to be fair, in the beginning, it wasn't. In another 10 years people might marvel that there was ever a time when businesses ignored social media (or its replacement concept) altogether. That might even be seen as a quaint, somewhat old fashioned time in our world's history. Remember paper calendars? Or telephones with cords?

How Does PR Work?

There are any number of ways to conduct an online PR program for your business.

When my company establishes one for a client, we look at our client's goals and go from there. There needs to be a strategy and it needs to involve consistency.

Often we will develop a press release campaign that sees a new press release developed every two months on issues that will likely resonate with our client's customers and peers.

We know that the more newsworthy the topic, the more attention the release will get, so we are always at pains to ensure the press releases are not fluffy announcements about the company baseball tournament – unless, of course that tournament raised a substantial amount of money for charity, perhaps.

Working with our clients, we develop a press distribution list that targets the industry organizations and news outlets that are important to our client and their customers, or we might make use of one of the press distribution services that will look after distribution to thousands of outlets around the world.

Any queries the releases generate are funneled to one of our client's representatives for answering.

Most traditional publications post their content to their online site and the editorial team may or may not be different for each venue. Ideally you want the real name of a real person to whom you can address your request for attention.

Here are some ideas for the type of online channel to which you might send your release:

- The websites of industry organizations or associations to which you belong
- Websites that specialize in that area
- Forums that are focused on your industry or topic
- The blogs of people who write a lot about your topic
- The social media accounts of people or organizations that specialize in your area
- Google Plus: events, hangouts and other groups that focus on your area of specialization
- LinkedIn groups

If that sounds like too much effort, or you don't have time, you can also look into any one of a number of newswire services available that, for a fee, will distribute your press release for you.

These organizations have extensive lists of publications in every field around the world and they claim to update the contact information for all editors and community managers regularly. If you purchase their service, they will send your release out for you, and track the response you triggered with a report back to you on how many impressions you generated.

As with other forms of content marketing, messaging is key in online PR. We want the messages about the company to be consistent with what we are saying in other venues and it all needs to drive to the ultimate value our client offers to their customers.

There need to be regular planning meetings to determine what topics we're going to cover in our press campaign and that usually revolves around an editorial calendar that dovetails with the other activities our clients are engaged in throughout the year.

Surprises happen – when one of our clients buys another company, for example, we need to interrupt scheduled programming to bring out the big news. But, generally speaking, we follow a schedule.

When you're working with a marketing company, by the way, it's a good idea to meet regularly with the team assigned to your account.

There are a lot of details involved in running a marketing program and much as you feel a great deal of trust for the people who are running your marketing programs (and we hope you do!), it's important that a clear communications channel exists to ensure messaging is as powerful as possible and problems are avoided.

Plus it's true that marketing can be very complex and the more you understand about what people are doing on your behalf, the more control you will have over the outcome. Nobody knows your business the way you do and the challenge for your marketing team lies in ensuring they communicate your priorities in as powerful and enticing a way as possible to the people with whom you want to do business.

A public relations program can be a lot of work and it can take a lot of focused effort to ensure that your message is crafted and broadcast in ways that will be heard by your ideal customers. But it's a very practical tool and, done well, it's an opportunity to create an impact that far outweighs the cost of developing a program around its maintenance.

PR has been around for a long time now. And although it might adjust to the changing platforms for its use, it's going to be with us for a long time to come. And it still represents a great opportunity for your business to shine.

Action You Can Take Today:

1. Make a list of 10 news or industry publications where you would like to see your company's news appear.
2. Check out each one's "Submission Guidelines" for press releases.
3. Make a list of five potential topics around which you could write a press release about your business. Make sure they focus on real "news."
4. Ask your marketing manager or, if you don't have one, hire a writer, to draft a press release.
5. Send the release to the publications you've selected.
6. Track whether or not your release was posted – follow up with an email or telephone call if desired.
7. Rinse and repeat.

Chapter Thirteen
Search Engine Optimization

I remember the wave of panic that hit me when I first came across the letters "SEO." I had no clue what they stood for and no idea why I should care. Even worse, I had a sinking feeling that they were probably Terribly Important.

Nobody I talked to at the time knew what those infernal letters meant and so, for a while, I carried blithely on with my writing expecting them to go away. They didn't.

As a writer I had seen plenty of acronyms along the way. I've done a lot of work in the fields of journalism, government and corporate communications and PR, and I was used to the jargon that people familiar with a topic like to throw around in place of clear communication. There's no point judging it… but acronyms need to be explained.

Young reporters run into a Law in Journalism that says if you don't spell out an acronym on first reference, and then put the acronym in brackets beside the words the letters represent, then you are going to go to Writer Hell in the form of a good tongue lashing from the editor in charge of editing your story.

Once you've been taught that rule, you have to follow it or risk the wrath of the Angels of Editorial Vengeance.

While I no longer live in fear of an editor, or the angels who do their dirty work for them, this does strike me as a pretty good rule to follow. If you don't provide people with an explanation for an acronym you are closing the door to a private club you don't actually want anyone else to join.

I find that digital marketing experts do tend to keep those doors closed. There are a lot of acronyms flying around this world and at the time I first ran into the aforementioned "SEO" term, I had no clue that it was going to change my life.

I make no pretense of being an early adopter here, but when you are a marketing copywriter and you sniff something in the air that you think is going to revolutionize how marketing writing is going to be done, it's a good idea to sit up and pay attention.

So I did.

As a writer focused on building a business in an evolving online universe, I nervously jumped into the oceans of online information available on Search Engine Optimization and tried to learn how to swim in it.

And although I'm still surfing the ever-evolving waves of change in this field, I've become a huge student of SEO. It's an incredibly elegant field of study.

In simple terms, Search Engine Optimization (SEO) is a marketing strategy designed to help your organization rank at or near the top of the millions of listings that crop up when someone searches for what you have to offer.

The closer your website listing is to the top of the list, the more likely it is that your perfect client is going to be able to find you and click through to your website.

Your website is usually your premier vehicle for starting conversations with the people who might want to buy what you are selling.

So your website needs to be in good shape and your strategy for leading people to it needs to be in good shape as well. You can educate yourself on how to do all that — I invested thousands of dollars and countless hours in my own education on the topic, and many other people have done that too.

There is a lot I could be doing better and with unlimited time and money I would be doing all of it. And then I would watch it all change again within six months.

But we know it's possible to learn what needs to be learned to have an edge in this world. Or you can hire people to do it all for you. Which can also be pricey. But either way, if you want to be found online, your website needs to be optimized.

That may not be a goal of yours, by the way. I know plenty of business people who are happy to use their website as a brochure, rather than a business generator, especially in view of the time and money it can cost to haul that website into state-of-the-SEO-art perfection. And especially in view of the fact that your website is going to be hopelessly out of date in three years anyway.

There is a limit to what a small business can spend on its internet presence and although a lot of internet marketers will try to shame you into tearing your website down and starting over, I am not one of those people who is going to get sniffy about how awful your website is.

You probably know that your website isn't serving you well.

You don't need me to embarrass you into changing it. I assume that if you had the money, people resources, knowledge and/or time, you would be thrilled to launch a new website.

But are there a few things you could be doing better? I'm thinking yes. Because I hate to think that you're missing an opportunity to make more money.

What Does SEO Involve?

Good SEO involves specific off- and on-site behaviours that work together to convince the search engines that you are credible, reliable and relevant to your customers.

The goal is to rank ever higher in the Search Engine Results Pages (SERPs).

A lot of SEO has traditionally revolved around the effective use of "keywords " — terms your desired clients use when they are searching for what you offer.

Finding the right keywords can take quite a bit of research, but they are important to successful SEO — a lot less so than they used to be, but even that may change over the next few months and years.

From an off-site perspective, at this point in time, you need as many links to your website as possible from other credible websites, and ideally the description of your organization on those off-site links will include language built around your keywords.

Your on-site strategy is a little more complicated as it involves much more finesse around such issues as the architecture of your site, the coding, the use of title tags (the words that show up in the bar running across the top of a web page) and last but not least, the content of your website itself.

The most important thing to remember is to use your keywords consistently in everything you write.

It's probably a good idea to use them in your headlines and in the text of every page. They're there for one purpose only: to signal to the search engine "crawlers" the fact that your website is a perfect match for the keywords your ideal client just used to call up information from the Internet.

The challenge is to write your content around your keywords in a way that engages the people reading it. While good SEO will generate visitor traffic, what happens when people get to your website is entirely up to you.

If their experience is marred by ugly visuals, lack of contextual cues, poor writing or insufficient information, or if they're turned off by a ham-fisted display of nothing but keywords, then you've lost the chance to draw them more deeply into your marketing funnel. No engagement, no conversation, no sale.

As SEO evolves, we're finding that engagement is by no means limited to the words you use, either: in fact, information I obtained from Canada News Wire (CNW) shows that news releases that make use of photos, video and other forms of multimedia get a whopping 77% more views than those that use text alone.

More views mean a greater possibility of converting those folks into customers and supporters.

As an entrepreneur and avid student of this powerful marketing tool, I'm always on the lookout for ways to build my business.

It took a lot of dedicated effort for me to learn what I needed to know in order to ensure my SEO and content strategies worked well together.

And there are many things my business could be doing to improve how we do this. If the days were longer, if the weeks were less hectic, if we had more employees with not enough to do, if there were free funding available... annnnnd if pigs could fly, we would have a perfect SEO strategy and our execution would be flawless.

But we are a small business making choices just like everyone else and the key point is that our strategy is working well enough to continue growing the business at a pace we can barely handle.

Searching, searching...

This isn't technically a book about SEO and there are people out there who are far better equipped than I am to wax poetic about the "how-to's" of the topic.

The interesting thing is, you could easily write an entire book about SEO and it would be probably be pretty much completely out of date 18 months after you set out to write it.

My staff and I have invested hundreds and hundreds and hundreds of hours in learning about it and practising it, and we are still moving towards the granular, perhaps cellular, understanding that would certify us as SEO Nerds.

But what we often talk about (among lots of other stuff) is that, despite the fact that SEO is a moving target (algorithms change and people's online behaviour changes, etc.), high quality links are still important for SEO.

What That Means is This:

As I mentioned, the search engines are continuously crawling the web looking at the endless crush of information that people are piling into it at the rate of trillions of bytes a minute.

They need to find a way to figure out what it all means and they need a way to determine which information is important for what purpose. That helps them give suggestions for sites to the people who are searching for something.

They make that determination in a number of ways, and one of the most important ones lies in assessing "what else" has connections to the information — say we're talking about your website.

If that "what else" happens to be a number of dead end links or poorly ranked websites, or if there aren't *any* links connecting to your website at all, then the search engines are going to feel that your website isn't very important and they will rank it poorly.

If your website has links connecting it to some highly ranked and very important websites, however, such as an established and important media outlet or industry organization, then the search engines will think "Ahhhh, this website is important!"

On deeming your website is important, the search engines will then give it a few more points in the algorithm that determines ranking.

You will float a little higher in search engine results when people are looking for what you offer.

An easy way to do that is with a press campaign – the more releases you produce, and the more pick-up you get, the better you rank, the more likely your ideal customers are to find you and the more money you have the opportunity of making. (We talked more about this in Chapter 12)

That's the simplified version of the story.

In reality there are a lot of other issues that go into good SEO, and ranking well is the result of a collection of other activities that also seem to be related to the phase of the moon and the roll of the dice.

It's quite a scientific process.

And sometimes it doesn't seem that scientific at all.

Quite honestly, that could change tomorrow.

More Information

If you want a lot more information about this topic I recommend you check out the Google Search Engine Optimization Starter Guide at this link:

http://static.googleusercontent.com/media/www.google.com/en//webmasters/docs/search-engine-optimization-starter-guide.pdf

It is an excellent resource that provides a great deal of basic information about:

- Creating page titles
- Using "description" meta tags
- Improving your website's structure
- Improving the structure of your URLs
- Making your site easier to navigate
- Optimizing your content
- Offering quality content and services
- Writing anchor text
- Optimizing images
- Using heading tags appropriately
- Using robots.txt
- SEO for Mobile Phones
- Promoting your website correctly
- Using free webmaster tools

Here are a few more links that might also be helpful:

Google's blog about how to improve your website: http://googlewebmastercentral.blogspot.com/

The Google Webmaster Central Blog: http://www.google.com/support/webmasters/

Information on Google's Webmaster Tools:

http://www.google.com/webmasters/guidelines.html

Google Analytics: http://www.google.com/analytics/

I also recommend Hubspot's eBook, ***25 Must-Haves for Driving Traffic, Leads and Sales,*** which you can access through this link: http://offers.hubspot.com/25-website-must_haves-for-driving-traffic-leads-and-sales.

And, of course, if you feel you would like to discuss more about how high quality content can help you improve your SEO, then please contact me at:

susan@crossmancommunications.com.

Action You Can Take Today:

Review the links that I've provided in this chapter and decide if:

- a) You feel SEO is important enough to investigate further
- b) You believe your business needs to implement an SEO strategy
- c) You would like to speak with me directly about how Crossman Communications can support you in your efforts to improve your Search Engine Optimization

Chapter Fourteen
Measurement

It's all well and good to develop a fancy-shmancy content marketing program that has your competitors gnashing their teeth and crying into their pillows at night – but how do you know if it's actually working?

The short answer is, "You measure it."

The longer answer is much more complicated than that. Measurement is an important part of your content marketing program but there are many different ways to measure your content marketing initiatives; the problem, as I see it, is that you could invest an enormous amount of company time, energy and money in a measurement program and totally miss the fact that your program is actually working – at least in some areas.

Marketing generally is sometimes considered a bit of a mystery zone.

While the folks in the sales department can point to hard numbers that relate to their effort and their results, the marketing people can't always pin down which of their many channels convinced someone to come to your website and take a look.

Someone might link to the home page of your website directly from your Twitter channel and then go straight to your "Contact Us" page to get in touch.

But maybe they had also already:

- seen your company's booth at a tradeshow a few years ago
- begun receiving your e-newsletter a year-and-a-half ago
- been watching your activity on Facebook for six months
- participated in one of your free webinars
- followed your company on LinkedIn and
- noticed that you showed up on Page 2 of the Search Engine Results Pages (SERPs) when they were looking for something related to what you sell

Which marketing channel gets to take credit for starting the conversation that might lead to a sale?

We might be tempted to give it to the Twitter feed. But is that fair?

It's been said for years, decades even; that it takes a good 13 exposures to your brand before someone who needs what you offer will take action to get in touch.

Of course, the point at which they get in touch also depends on where they are in the sales cycle – have they only recently become aware of their need or are they actively researching options to fulfill it?

Perhaps they've narrowed the choice of supplier down to three companies. People can circle around a company's online presence for a l-o-n-g time before they do anything that will bring them closer.

So the marketing people can capture a certain amount of information related to their numbers, but not always all of it; accuracy can be elusive.

Meanwhile, the sales people know that they placed 200 calls, connected with 40 people, booked nine visits and made four sales that brought the company $20,000. The sales involved four lunches, $85 in gas money and the cost of a $35 book a prospect was interested in reading that the salesperson bought as a gift.

Add to all of that, the portion of the salesperson's hourly wage that went into landing the deal and you have a full set of pretty numbers that tell the whole story. Calculating a return on investment (ROI) in sales is a comparatively simple and easily quantifiable effort.

We can still calculate an ROI in marketing. But it's not always possible to know which element of your online content had the most impact on an individual's decision to email you or pick up the phone and call.

We might know where they were when the purchase trigger was pulled. But the path they followed could be tortuous.

That being said, it is highly desirable to do what it takes to show up well in search engine results. For that you need a highly appealing and optimized website, and enough online presence and activity to convince the search engines that they need to push you to page one of the SERPs. Page three at a pinch.

But how does that work?

We've all done website searches and started sorting through the results that the search engine results gave us.

We've found a web page listing that looked appealing and linked to that company's website. It showed up in the first place because that company possibly/probably had active presences on Twitter, Google+, Facebook, YouTube and LinkedIn, and their consistent messaging across all platforms indicates that they sell what you need.

So the number of website visits that company gets is directly related to how well it is maximizing its online real estate overall. The matrix is expanding and I think businesses now need to measure as much as possible and become so familiar with their statistics that they get a good feel for which activities are co-related with more queries.

But I'm getting a little ahead of myself.

The basic message I want to get across here is that you need to know what you want to measure and to do that (if we can step back for a moment), you need to know what your content marketing goals are. This is only logical. If you set a goal and take action anywhere in life, and then measure your results, you can adjust your action in the future to try to achieve different results.

But without the goal, there's no way of knowing whether your results are good or bad, and there's no way to know what to improve going forward.

Content marketing programs can become very pricey. They are, at times, somewhat labour intensive and, to be honest, a consultant with enough expertise to think they know what they're doing (to the extent that this field lends itself to overarching expertise) is not going to work for peanuts.

You can find people who will work cheaply, and you can find writers on crowdsourcing sites like Elance or Fiverr who will write a page of copy for a handful of dollars. A lot of people I respect a great deal in the digital space highly recommend this route. I'm not yet convinced that you can get great quality for a low price through these sites.

Do you want to put your reputation in the hands of someone who is so desperate for work that they will labour for a price that is well below the North American minimum wage?

Especially since they possibly don't speak your language well, and have virtually zero knowledge of or understanding about your business? You might save dollars on the outlay, but it's going to cost you dollars on the in-come. Writing is an area of craftsmanship. You get what you pay for.

So when a new client comes to my company asking to deliver "some content marketing," one of the very first questions we ask is, "Why? What is it you want to achieve?" And we develop a program around those goals.

Every customer has different objectives. Some want better search engine results. Some want more visitors to their website. Others want more engagement on Twitter. Still others just want to improve their online reputation because they are planning to sell their company and they need to establish a larger online presence in order to support a higher price.

And, if you drill down to the "whys" of the matter, you will probably find that a company's goals relate to expanding the number of prospects and customers they have, supporting the purchase process and strengthening relationships with a community.

What's more, every answer should, in most cases, ultimately drill down to the fact that we are trying to make money here.

What's the impact of all this content marketing noise on the bottom line?

I invite you to be wary of the marketing world to some extent: marketers usually love this stuff. We love the processes and we love the elegance of the digital world. We love website development and we love building communities. A lot of us love metrics and a lot of us love words, images and audio clips.

We are enchanted by consumer behaviour and we are intrigued by where marketing is going.

There are whole magazines that follow the careers of up and comers in the marketing world. We are immersed in the actions we take and the knowledge we have.

But if we and you can't keep the end dollars in mind, we shouldn't play this game. At the end of the day, for most Business-to-Business (BtoB) — and most Business-to-Consumer (BtoC) businesses, content marketing is about making money.

In some cases, such as that of organizations with a charitable objective, it might be about influencing behaviour. But there still need to be goals that relate to measurable results. You can't improve what you don't measure.

The data you gather with your content marketing initiative might relate to any number of criteria and measurement can get quite complicated. Typically, though, we look at:

Number of website visits

Ideally you want this number to go up over time regardless of what your other objectives might be.

At the same time, you want your bounce rate to go down. Your bounce rate measures the percentage of site visitors who arrived on your site and left without visiting more than one page.

A high bounce rate indicates lack of engagement with your material. This might be because a lot of your visitors were searching for something specific that the search engines indicated they would find on your website. When the human visitor got there, they didn't find it, or perhaps they weren't immediately certain that they *would* find it, so they left.

So, for example, if you make bakery equipment and someone was looking for a countertop mixmaster, your company might show up in the search engine results page (SERP) for a "mixmaster" search.

The searcher might click on your listing, get to your site, see the giant mixer in the image on your front page and think "Oh this is *so* not what I'm looking for," and leave right away. That's a bounce.

A high bounce rate might also stem from the fact that a lot of visitors found the subject matter they were looking for on your site, but they were so turned off by your presentation that they left. This could mean that it's time for a new site.

(As a side note here, I wouldn't worry too much if your bounce rate is over 40%, or even 50%. But if it's north of 70% you definitely need to do some fine-tuning).

Page Rank

One of the very important aspects of content marketing is that it is an extremely important way to boost your search engine rankings. There are people out there promoting the idea that you need to use massive amounts of verbiage to get you Googling well. But make no mistake: if the real human visitors to your site don't understand what you're telling them, then you won't make the sale. They'll bounce off your site faster than a superball.

According to the brilliant content marketing expert Neil Patel, web pages that rank on page one of Google typically have between 2,032 and 2,494 words – and ensuring that your web pages are filled with detailed, useful content will increase the chances that your business will rank higher with search engines.

He also notes that companies with blogs typically receive 97% more leads than companies without blogs because content-rich sites usually get more back links and social traffic, helping them generate more traffic overall:

(Source: http://www.quicksprout.com/2014/02/06/how-content-marketing-affects-search-engine-rankings/).

This also makes intuitive sense: if you are consistently adding interesting, relevant content to your website, you are adding more opportunities for the search engines to crawl your site and assess your site's value to visitors.

A site with limited, static, content does not have nearly the appeal of a site with a lot of variety.

It's important to note, however, that this is what the state of the art is today. The net is an ever-evolving creature and the algorithms that search engines like Google and others use to determine rank change over time.

Conventions change. Staying on top of it all takes a lot of focus!

Number of Followers, Fans, Connections or Likes on Social Media:

When I first got involved in social media I developed a strategy and peeked at my stats proudly every week to see how many new connections I had made. I watched my Twitter followers grow from none to 100 pretty quickly and I enthusiastically kept tweeting away as the numbers grew: 123, 147, 199, oh if only I could crack 200! It was a thrilling time.

I was likewise bursting with excitement when my LinkedIn followers surpassed 250. And when I surpassed that magical 500 mark, I felt like a somebody!

And what I completely missed, as a newbie, was the answer to the question "Why do I want the numbers to grow?" It was all very good to put strategies in place to increase my number of followers and the like, but the point of it all was... what?

Oh yes, like *any* form of marketing that has surfaced on the planet over the past 100,000 years or so, the point of *online* marketing is to start conversations with the people who need what you're selling.

And it does work. When all the wheels of the Crossman Communications marketing machine are rolling in the same direction, we can have two or three requests for phone consultations coming in every week.

We are a small company that delivers a highly customized service. A larger company, and one that needs to sell massive numbers of their product or service, will want to be doing a multiple of that number (and there are ways to do that) but, for us, that's a very good way to fill our marketing funnel.

We have strategies that we implement among a company's sales force to teach them how to use LinkedIn for lead generation and if you're interested in that kind of a project, please let me know.

Not all of the queries we or our clients get are perfectly well-qualified, and, frankly, part of what happens in a telephone conversation is to determine if we are a good fit. I'm OK with that. (Those people know people who know people...)

But guess what? Part of the reason we have consistent opportunities to speak with people who might want what we're selling is that we have grown our community and we are regularly communicating with the members of it.

This stuff works!

Open and Click Through Rates for Email Marketing Campaigns

I went into a fair bit of detail about email marketing campaigns in earlier in this book (see Chapter 11) so I don't want to repeat myself too much here.

But if we can review the topic for just a moment, it's worth stressing that it's important to measure both the open rates and the click through rates of your email marketing campaigns.

The open rate quite simply measures the percentage of email recipients who saw your email in their inbox and opened it. You want this number to be as high as possible, above 20 per cent if possible.

There are benchmarks available online for different industries and you can check the average for your field and see how well you're tracking against it.

A lot of issues affect your open rate, including your subject line (again, simple is better), the day and time your email was sent, and the size and sourcing of your list.

The click through rate measures the number of people who clicked a link in the email you sent them to go on and visit whatever online presence you selected. This is ideally a page of your website.

We often set up specific landing pages to drive people to take an action we would like them to take – sign up for a free eBook, download a free audio, etc.

You want your click through rate to be as high as possible as well, but don't expect massive numbers here – generally we see rates in the neighbourhood of 2-4%, although it can be higher with a great offer and a well defined list.

Most email marketing delivery systems will track both the open rate and the click through rate for you so you can fine tune your efforts and get higher rates.

Click through rates are not just applicable to emails, however. If you are doing any online PR or advertising you also want to measure your click-throughs.

Engagement

Are people engaging with your online content? It's highly desirable to generate the involvement of the community you build online and that's one way to measure whether or not they find your messaging and your offer appealing.

For example, are people commenting on or sharing your blog posts? Or retweeting, favouriting or responding to your tweets?

Are you getting lots of shares on your Facebook posts and LinkedIn updates?

Expanding your engagement means extending your reach. The more people who hear what you have to say, the greater your potential for starting the conversations that can lead to a sale.

A Word on Your Return on Investment

It's generally noted in the content marketing world that, as I mentioned earlier, results can be tricky to track to content marketing. Whole departments are sometimes devoted to tracking results.

As a small company, it can be difficult to measure. If you have downloadable materials (white papers, webinars, templates, etc.) on your website you can at least track how many people provided their information and how many ultimately turned into customers through that channel.

Ideally, you want to continue communicating with people after they have downloaded your free material. What else can you offer them? How else can you keep in touch? And you want to track the cost of turning them from a prospective customer into an actual customer.

So, for example, if your content marketing this year cost you $100,000 and you followed the trail of potential customer behaviours and exposures to find out that the leads generated through the content marketing initiatives alone increased your sales by $145,000, then you can calculate your ROI this way:

$$\frac{\$145{,}000 - \$100{,}000}{\$100{,}000} = \frac{\$45{,}000}{\$100{,}000} = 45\%$$

In reality, it's often difficult to determine where a lead came from, and how many exposures they've actually had to your online content. That being said, the downloadable materials make it possible to track at least the leads that came through that channel, and where they go from there. Most businesses that want to use their content to generate more sales will find that it takes nine months or more to get set up and into a position where measureable results are achievable. Some content marketers suggest that it's really only after a year that results begin to show up. Other types of digital marketing can get results faster but they are not usually related to brand development, reputation management, or information cultivation. Amazon best seller campaigns, for example, can generate hundreds of book sales in one day by employing highly complex and well-organized strategies.

They are not relying on their content to drive sales, however, and they are usually a B to C, rather than a B to B concept.
Most of Crossman Communications' clients want a content marketing strategy in place because they realize they need to tell their story in engaging and effective ways. They want the people who visit their online properties to know what they do, and they want to develop some rapport with them so that they are motivated, as much as is possible, to embark upon a business relationship with them.

This is story-telling at its most technical. The stories we tell ourselves influence the results we get, in business and in life, and the stories we tell our potential customers are likewise crucial to results. Measuring the effect of our story telling lets us know if we need to be telling better stories.

Action You Can Take Today:

- Make a list of goals for your content marketing program.
- Determine what kind of content is likely to support those goals.
- Determine what metrics you need to measure in order to determine if your program is working.
- Set up your program.
- Start measuring
- Reach out to Crossman Communications at: susan@crossmancommunications.com if you need help putting a content marketing program together.

Chapter Fifteen
Tools

Every tradesman needs a set of tools and content marketing provides no exception to the rule. The internet is a vast playground, and the range of activity you can undertake within it is virtually unlimited. And, as the internet has become more complex, the tools to streamline content marketing have expanded as well, to the point now where one almost needs at least one full-time employee to track, assess and implement the tools needed to do this all with the greatest efficiency possible.

I can remember how delighted I was to discover a social media management tool called "Hootsuite" a number of years ago. It revolutionized how I had been tracking my social media efforts and it streamlined posting, as well. This platform allows you to coordinate all of your social media platforms from one central dashboard. You can post to your platforms, upload photos, monitor your news feeds and respond to people's comments without having to ping-pong back and forth from one platform to another.

Years after we first discovered it, my team still finds Hootsuite a valuable tool: it has stayed relevant despite the fact that our business needs have grown dramatically; it's proven a great choice for our team. But Hootsuite is just one of countless other tools available to facilitate the set up, operation and assessment of a content marketing program. And, in fact, the number and variety of tools available can be bewildering— new ones are being added almost daily—so it's probably not a bad idea to add them to your tool chest one at a time.

Why Bother With Tools?
Using at least some of the content marketing tools available on line is a key part of succeeding with your content marketing. Tools can help you save time and effort, of course, but they are also an important way to:

- Determine whether or not you are meeting your goals
- Determine what you need to do to fine tune your efforts
- Help you make sure you are spending your time and energy on relevant activities
- Save you money
- Develop strategies for future success

Some tools are, of course, more helpful for some people than they are for others. Just to give you a sense of the number of tools available, check out this list of tools made available by a company called Curata: http://www.curata.com/blog/content-marketing-tools-ultimate-list/. It's mind-boggling how many tools are out there—and this is by no means an exhaustive list! Most tools are designed to improve efficiency and effectiveness and it's worth investigating a few of them to find ways of streamlining your content efforts.

The "Big Daddy" of Tools
Yes, I'm talking about Google Analytics. There are other analytics packages out there that many will agree are more effective than Google Analytics, and there are numerous "user error" issues that will affect your results, but this one is free, fairly comprehensive and it will give you reasonably good information about what you might need to do to improve your marketing results. It comes with a warning, however: you just might get hooked on analytics.

One of the very important aspects of content marketing is that it is an extremely important way to boost your search engine rankings. There are people out there promoting the idea that you use massive amounts of verbiage to get you Googling well. But make no mistake: if the real human visitors to your site don't understand what you're telling them, then you won't make the sale. They'll be gone and you will be eating their dust.

Every person who has a website can have that website registered for free with Google Analytics. When you log into your account, you will be able to look at mountains of information about how many people have been coming to your website, what pages they viewed, how long they stayed, where they were online before they got to your site, what country they're from, what language they speak and on and on and on.

Why is that important? It's important because you can learn what parts of your content marketing strategy are working well and which ones need fine tuning just by looking at the Google Analytics information. If you have very few visitors to your site, and they are bouncing off almost as soon as they get there, then you probably need to beef up your other online properties and give people a compelling reason to visit your website while improving the content you have on the site itself.

If you have a lot of visitors to your site, and they are coming from a lot of other online locations, but your visitors bounce off your site on the home page, then you need to look at what you're offering and how well you're targeting your ideal clients. It's a very complex topic area. Of course, all of this helps improve your search engine optimization (SEO) results, which feeds directly into your efforts to funnel visitors to your site.

I resisted learning about my analytics for a Very Long Time. I'm a writer, not a mathematician, and for years I self-identified as "Bad At Numbers." Why on Earth would I want to belabour the point by subjecting myself to the humiliation of struggling with an Analytics account?! Even in university I took the easiest statistics course on campus and the fact that I somehow managed to pull off an "A" did nothing to make a love of statistics blossom in my heart. Those were the days when a computer took up an entire room and we had to spend hours painstakingly punching our code into stacks of cards to run a program whose purpose escaped me entirely.

Businesses didn't have websites and how delightful it is for me today, by contrast, to first of all have a website to play with and, second of all to be able to easily find out how people are experiencing it: I open a browser, type in a url and select a topic about which I want to learn more. The information shows up and all I have to do is look at it and think about it. Easy peasy!

Somewhere along the road between "I hate numbers" to "I love analytics" I had an epiphany: numbers point the way to improvement. Full stop. So even for writers like me, who adore language and struggle with formulae, there is a really good reason for becoming immersed in statistics and that reason comes right down to Revenue Generation.

When we first walk into the Google Analytics (GA) accounts of most of our clients we know that we will be dealing with something that looks like a squirrel got trapped in it. That's not a criticism – stewardship of these accounts passes from one person to the next in an organization. Here's how that might look:

- Sally, the receptionist, set up the GA account five years ago and when it seemed too complicated she handed over authority after six months to George, the company's General Manager

- George is Six Sigma Black Belt certified with an MBA but he has much more pressing concerns than managing the company's GA reports so when the company hired Jane as a marketing assistant, he gave her responsibility for organizing it all

- Jane left the company to move to Edmonton and there was no-one in the job until the company hired us to handle its content marketing

- When we arrived on the scene we found that there were five email accounts affiliated with the GA account and nothing had been effectively set up, managed or monitored probably since forever. The account administrator turned out to be the receptionist who had left the company a long time ago for parts unkown. This has an impact on the company's Google+ account, as well as its YouTube account but aside from all that, it means we have a fair bit of work to do.

When it's properly set up, however, Google Analytics provides a massive amount of information about what's happening on your website every minute of every day. Your analytics can tell you, for example:

- how many people are visiting your site, and when
- where they are geographically located
- what language they speak
- what kind of browser they used to access your site
- whether they used a mobile device or a desktop device when visiting your site
- what pages they have visited on any one visit and how long they stayed each time
- how people arrived on your site (through a social media or other link, via a search engine query or by typing your url directly into their browser)

- whether your visitors have visited your site multiple times
- The age and gender breakdown of your site visitors
- Much, much more

It's great to know all that information. But what do you do with it?

We talked in the last chapter about how measuring the number of visitors to your website is one of the indicators of how well your content marketing strategy is working. Your Analytics will give you a lot of that information. What's more, say you've been posting a blog once a month and your analytics indicate that every time you do that the number of visitors to your website increases by 20%. Well, it would make sense to post more blogs, wouldn't it?

Analytics and Blog Posts
So you start posting a blog once a week, you drive people to it via social media, you maybe put a link to your blog in your email signature, and eventually you notice that you've built the number of visitors to your website up by a substantial amount. Kudos! Now you look a little deeper at your analytics and you realize that every time you posted a blog about how you solved a unique customer problem, your statistics improved: you got more visitors, they stayed longer on your site, and they browsed more pages.

What else can you do with that?

First of all, why not write more blogs about customer problem-solving? People are obviously interested in the topic, so you want to capitalize on it. You could write a five-post series on the top five most common problems your company solves for your customers and, once that's done, turn the series into a white paper that people can download in exchange for their email address (so you can build your email marketing list). You could call your white paper "The Five Most Expensive Problems in _____ ("X" area)...and How to Solve Them." You could include an offer in your white paper for a free consultation or some sort of marketing incentive to encourage people to continue their conversation with you.

And you would want to measure the responses you get on all fronts.

Analytics and Acquisition
In looking at your analytics maybe you realize that hardly any people are coming to your website as a result of an organic search. An organic search is when a potential customer goes looking for something they need online and in so doing they type a search term into their search engine window. They will get hundreds of thousands, if not millions, of results.

The websites listed in the first couple of pages are the ones they are most likely to visit. If you have not invested much time, energy or money in your search engine optimization strategy (SEO), your website will not show up in those first few pages and people will not know about what you have to offer.

It's great to have a pretty website. It's even better if people can find it, visit it and feel motivated after visiting it to start a conversation with you that might lead to a sale.

Many business owners I speak with are content with a website that they feel represents them reasonably well and there is certainly some merit in that very piece. But if your competition has gone the extra mile and is showing up on Page One of the search engine results pages, and you are not, then you are obviously not capitalizing on the opportunity that exists for you. And your analytics will tell you if there is room for improvement in this area.

Suffice to say that you can get ample information from your Analytics data to determine how well your optimization efforts are going. If you see from your Analytics that most of the visitors to your website are coming direct, i.e. by typing your url into a web browser, but hardly anyone is coming via an organic search, then you know you have some work to do.

If 65% of your visits are directed to you by organic search, but they have a high bounce rate, then you should probably do some fine tuning to determine why they're leaving so quickly. It's all information and the possibility for improving is always there.

There is an awful lot more in Google Analytics that can be helpful and we've really just scratched the surface here. But it really is important and it's an amazing tool for improving your online marketing.

Here's another example of how a tool can be helpful: www.Tweepsmap.com

When I first started using Twitter I would monitor the Crossman Communications Twitter feed manually. I would log in to my Twitter account, add followers one by one, and respond to direct messages through the platform itself. This could be time consuming. There are a lot of different ways to use Twitter for business and one of the beliefs I have about that platform is that it's generally a good idea to have a higher number of followers than people who you are following.

And, there are a lot of people in your Twitter community with whom you are probably never going to do business. They are not in your target audience and they don't offer a service you need or desire. Possibly they also opened a Twitter account two years ago, gathered 300 followers, sent out 11 tweets and then haven't touched the platform since. You are clearly not going to have much opportunity to start a conversation that might lead to a sale with those people. And it's unlikely that they will add to your overall quality of life in any way.

So there is no compelling reason to follow them. You want to fill your Twitter funnel with the people and businesses that are going to contribute to your well-being and with whom you might have a productive and profitable relationship. Getting rid of clutter is an important part of that process.

It was fairly easy to track our followers when there were only a few hundred of them. But as time went on, and the account gained more traction, it became far too time consuming—and unprofitable—for us to weed through the Twitter account unfollowing the folks who were unlikely to become productive business connections.

And then along came Tweepsmap. Tweepsmap is an application that integrates with your Twitter account and provides a weekly report on what's happening on that platform. You can sign up for a free or a paid account, and, since we don't have a massive strategy on Twitter at this point, the free account is all we really need right now.

Tweepsmap tells us where our followers are located and what percentage are located in which countries. This is good information for a business to have: 42.2% of our Twitter followers are located in Ontario right now and 2.5% of them are located in Florida. Knowing this allows us to fine tune our offers and our language to maximize our appeal to those people who are most likely to do business with us. It can also queue us to say, "Hmmmm, we're not doing so well in Florida right now and we want to – why don't we fine tune our marketing strategy to give an extra incentive to people in Florida to follow us online?"

The free Tweepsmap account also lets us see who has unfollowed us recently and that gives us the option of unfollowing them in return or, if they are an important target for our marketing strategy, finding ways of communicating with them elsewhere. The platform tells us which Twitter accounts have not tweeted in six months and which ones have not tweeted in two months. If they are not active, and they are not a specific target, then, again, we have the option of eliminating them from our "Following" list. If a business is not active on Twitter, we are less likely to be able to connect with them or influence them on that platform.

The upshot is that this tool has become a great way to streamline our efforts on Twitter: we can stop following the accounts that are unlikely to bear business fruit so we can focus our messaging on the universe of people who are possibly potential clients, or their influencers. It's a very helpful tool!

www.Bitly.com
On the subject of Twitter, it takes a lot of skill to keep a post down to the 140 characters Twitter allows and one of the strategies around Twitter is to share links to content that your ideal clients and customers will find valuable. Some of those links are very long and unwieldy. Enter Bitly, which is a handy little link shortener that will take that 70-character link and shrink it down to 15 or 20 (or event seven or eight). It can be a little time consuming to take that extra step, but bitly certainly does streamline your links.

Portent Idea Generator for Writer's Block: http://www.portent.com/tools/title-maker
It's not always easy to come up with great titles for your content and when I stumbled across the Portent Idea Generator I have to say I was hooked. Enter any topic into the search box and this platform will develop off-the-wall ideas for a creative title that will certainly be memorable, if not usable. It strikes

me that the main value of this platform is not so much in getting a title for the blog post or article you are writing, but rather you are kick-starting a creative process that will allow you to come up with something that will please you.

The Screaming Frog SEO Spider:
http://www.screamingfrog.co.uk/seo-spider/
The Screaming Frog SEO Spider is a tool that lets you review a site from an SEO perspective so you can determine if everything is working that should be working. For example, say you linked from one of your blogs to a page that provides the details of a program you offer. Two years pass and you stop offering the program so you take down the page that invites people to sign up for it. The blog that sent people to the page about the program is now buried under 100 other blogs that followed and you have totally forgotten that you even wrote it. None of your staff members remember that you wrote it either. Because you disconnected that page, the blog is now host to a broken link, which search engines do not condone.

Maybe you have half a dozen other broken links that you don't even know exist. Maybe, for various other reasons, you even have 200 broken links. It can be very inefficient to shop a site and manually assess every single link on every single page and, actually, it's very unnecessary when you have the option of using a tool like Screaming Frog.

Screaming Frog will crawl your site for you and come back with a report about:

- Errors – Client errors such as broken links & server errors (No responses, 4XX, 5XX)

- Redirects – Permanent or temporary redirects (3XX responses)

- External Links – All external links and their status codes

- Protocol – Whether the URLs are secure (HTTPS) or insecure (HTTP)
- URL Issues – Non ASCII characters, underscores, uppercase characters, parameters, or long URLs
- Duplicate Pages
- Page Titles – Missing, duplicate, more than 65 characters, too short, etc.
- Meta Description – Missing, duplicate, more than 156 characters, too short, etc.
- Meta Keywords – Mainly for reference
- File Size – Size of URLs & images
- Response Time

This is a very useful tool and it's worth giving it a whirl so you get a good sense of what the search engines are seeing when they visit your site. They reward sites that are structured well and if yours is not, it could be holding you back from more traffic.

There are countless tools out there to streamline your content marketing efforts and I've mentioned just a few of our favourites. I'd love to hear about other ones that you have found valuable – please share your best with us on the Crossman Communications Facebook page!

Action You Can Take Today:

1. Make a list of the most frustrating aspects of managing online content.
2. List two actions you can take for each one that might lead to a happy conclusion.
3. Add each action to your calendar as a task
4. Take the action

Conclusion

I remember as a child glancing with a little wonder and just a touch of disgust at the Dick Tracy comic strip in what we used to call "The Funny Papers." Comics were an entertainment anchor for young people in those days, long before video games, Facebook and texting came along to abduct the attention span of children whose parents worked non-stop and were too exhausted to kick the kids outside to play. (And, yes, I fit in to that category now, too.)

Dick Tracy was, to me anyway, a relatively boring comic strip, with nowhere near the entertainment value of Blondie, Archie or The Family Circus.

There seemed to be a convoluted story involved in Dick Tracy's world that was way too serious and required a lot more attention than me, as an 11-year-old girl, was willing to spend on a newspaper. So I didn't pay it much heed. Other than to notice that Dick Tracy communicated with his boss through a watch-like gizmo that allowed them to see each other and talk to each other.

That was pretty cool.

It was an unthinkable gadget at the time and so ahead of its time that nobody thought it would ever actually be a possibility. This was long before cell phones arrived on the planet and, truth to tell, even long before fax machines and microwave ovens came along to give us the illusion that we were on the forefront of a technological "wave of the future."

A watch that allowed you to see someone? No way!

We might look at Dick Tracy's watch today and think "Oh, of course, Skype on a watch. Duuh. At some point, people are going to look at today's iWatches and think "how quaint, that was just before everybody started getting _____ watches that _____."

The point is, it's almost impossible to predict where digital marketing is headed and, indeed, what the implications for our social world are going to be. Anything is possible. We've all heard that if you can imagine it, you can create it, and many people reading this book today will be nodding their heads in agreement as they think of the business they are nudging forward so ferociously into a future they themselves can't quite picture.

The future is anybody's guess. And I think the important thing is not so much to be able to predict the future, as it is to be ready to roll with it.

You've been reading this book because you think the topic of content marketing is one that might be important for your business. If you're running a business right now, I salute you, because I know myself how challenging it can be to fit time to read into my day, and, also, how challenging it can be to take action. Business people aren't so much trying to "keep up with the Joneses" as they are trying to keep up with that demanding rascal, technology.

Content marketing is already old news and if you haven't started a content marketing program, you can no longer rush in to claim early adopter status. The good news, however, is that content marketing is still here and you can start taking advantage of the lessons the early adopters have learned along the way to keeping their businesses afloat. Is it time for you to take even a little bit of action to hook into a compelling future for your business?

Content marketing is, in fact, very old news. The original content marketing gurus used content unrelated to sales material to provide value to customers so they would associate something over and above a solid product with a company's brand name. In 1900 The Michelin Tire Company launched its famous "Michelin Guides" that now give travellers the skinny on the world's best restaurants. The Campbell's Soup Company produced its first cockbook in 1916 to give "housewives" ideas for using soup to make meals. Today, the company estimates that more than one million cans of soup are used in recipes every day:

(source: http://www.digitaldeliftp.com/LookAround/advertspot_campbells.htm).

In 1982 Hasbro partnered with Marvel Comics to develop the G.I. Joe Magazine. And although our concept of "content" has changed over the years, it's still that one stream of information we can create to inform, entertain, or intrigue people who just might do business with us. It's not designed specifically to trigger an immediate sale.

As entrepreneurs, we're pulled in a million different directions in an average day and it can be difficult to guarantee that we have the time available to do all the things we need to do in order to be successful.

One of our clients was very excited about the content marketing strategy someone had helped her set up and she had worked very hard at getting it all organized and scheduled. But at the point at which we came into her life, it had been six months since she had completed all of her organizational work, and she hadn't written her first blog post yet.

This happens to a lot of people because, not surprisingly, it takes quite a bit of time and attention to develop content and make sure it gets to the appropriate place online. If you haven't followed a content marketing strategy before, and you are trying to do it all yourself, you might find that it is very difficult to make yourself do the work. And, as content marketing strategists, my team and I are a drag on our clients' time. We require regular meetings so that we can get the information we need to both set up a program and implement it. We need to check in often with our clients to make sure we are representing them appropriately. And we seek approval on almost everything we post online so that our clients feel comfortable with how we are representing them.

We've recognized that there are some key "Summary Points" to keep in mind on your road to content marketing success and here are some of them:

1. Get in the habit of seeing your content marketing program as a high priority that adds a huge amount of value to your business. If you don't think it's important, you won't get to it. It takes a lot of consistency to make a content marketing program work. That needs to develop out of good habits.

2. Put your content marketing deadlines in your calendar and work to those deadlines. I write three or four blog posts at a sitting, more if I can, so I know they're ready to go. People get used to seeing your content show up online – you want to capitalize on that anticipation. Don't disappoint!

3. Outsource as much of your content management as you can. Your administrative assistant should be able to post your blog to your website and can format, and send out, your newsletter. If you are not a writer, hire someone to edit your blog posts and definitely hire someone to draft your white papers. While there's a little leeway in terms of professionalism in your blog posting, your white papers need to be top notch.

4. Be very clear as to who your audience is. You are not communicating with "everybody," you are marketing specifically to the people who might be interested in buying from you, OR their influencers. Good marketing is honest. In order to provide a program that unrolls with integrity, you want to take care to shine a light on your company's existing strengths, rather than "invent" ones that do not exist.

5. Make sure that your content references how your company solves client problems or eases their pain. Although other information needs to be there as well, it's important to stay focused on the reason for the content, which is to show that your organization is helpful, knowledgeable and focused on assisting customers to solve problems in the most cost-effective way possible. People are looking for value and they will be finding your online content while at different stages of the sales cycle. Your content should, ideally, reflect where they are in their deliberations.

6. Remember that this is a marathon, not a sprint – results take time. The more you do, and the longer you do it for, the more success you are going to enjoy. A content marketing program is sometimes something of a "build the plane as you fly it" kind of a proposition. New needs arise, and fine tuning your efforts is always a good idea. There are often a few bumps in the road as your business develops systems and fine tunes efficiencies.

7. It's important to remember that the tone of voice is important with content marketing – while online content typically requires a more conversational tone than a standard marketing brochure, for example, you want your content to be sensitive to how you want your company to be perceived—your brand should dictate how you are portrayed.

It can be hard for an entrepreneur to let go of the need to control every little detail and people often fear that bringing an outsider in to manage a content marketing program will somehow dilute their "voice." That is a very valid concern and I always recommend people hire the best talent they can afford in order to protect their reputation and further their business goals. That takes a fairly sophisticated business sense in itself, but the right writer — or videographer, or podcaster — will have the skills and the desire to present you in the absolute best light possible.

Trust is an important issue here. A great deal of time and energy has likely gone into building your company to where it is today and the last thing you need is to put your reputation in the hands of some social media yahoos who might just run it into the ground.

And, too, content marketing might be new to you. You're going to want to feel your way along for a while. My company, Crossman Communications, has been playing with marketing, social media and content for many years and although this is old news to us, we generally find that many of the projects we recommend for our clients are new to them.

In fact, we take great care to not only provide a service to our clients but to educate them about how content marketing works so that they can be partners in the process of tailoring their program to their product or service, their company culture, and, most importantly, their customer base.

Our clients tend to be people who are used to taking action and feeling the certainty that comes from having built a successful company; jumping into content marketing can be a very uncomfortable feeling for a lot of people and we take great pains to share our expertise as we work so that the unfamiliar becomes more "normal." There needs to be substantial collaboration and accountability in a content marketing program: regular meetings are key, as is a commitment to and a mechanism for communicating between meetings.

The relationship is important to us. Other outsourcing companies may work differently, and it's important that you feel you have a good fit with the people you are asking to help you sort through all this. Ask questions about how they see the relationship working.

Our team asks our new clients for a lot of information so that we can understand the matrix within which they operate. And initially, decisions need to be made on many issues.

Given that we are not insiders, there is something of a learning curve involved for our team as we learn the nuances of how our clients operate. Masses of information, much of which is second nature to our clients, need to be gathered, analyzed and acted upon. And, while we are reasonably quick learners, that does take some time.

We also tend to ask our clients to give some thought to what they need from us in order to feel confident that this program is being done "with," rather than "to" the company.

We are here to support our clients and how they feel we can best do that is important to us. And, while we provide as much analytical data as we can gather, there are other criteria that go into creating success. What are they for your company?

Finally, the program that we lay out for a customer is usually open to discussion. If there are elements that they feel will not serve them, we can make adjustments, although deleting any elements will usually dilute the results they are able to generate.

By the same token, if there is something they wish to see included that is not presented in one of our proposals, we can look at how that could be integrated into the program we have developed as well.

(And please contact me at: susan@crossmancommunications.com if you feel we can be of assistance here.)

Content marketing is a very elegant system and, done well, it will help you stand out from your competition and contribute to the generation of more leads and, therefore, more revenue. But for now, it's crucial that if you haven't already made the leap into content marketing, you do so as soon as you can, so you and your ideal customers can find each other in the delightful business of commercial transaction.

It's anybody's guess where the world of content is headed but it seems logical to me that there will be an increasing focus on analytics going forward and I also think there is going to be an increasing move towards micro communities.

As more and more companies dive into this beautiful world of online storytelling, it's going to be increasingly important for smaller businesses to learn how to develop a client community so they can create a virtual "place" for their clients to gather.

The big brands are already doing this, some of them very well, and it takes a lot of time — read investment — to make it happen.

I also think that video content will continue to be an important place for businesses moving forward.

The challenge is that it's going to continue to be tough for smaller businesses to create enough quality video content to make a big difference to their online presence. If video isn't done well, it doesn't reflect a business in the best light possible. While you can generate a piece of strong written content for $2,000 it takes at least 10 times that amount to create a strong piece of video content.

A cheap, poorly scripted, poorly written video with insufficient lighting and an inexperienced videographer behind the lens and an amateur editor in the cutting room can do more damage to your brand than good.

Aside from all, that, however, it seems to me that we can talk about the "future of content marketing" until we're blue but if your business has not already started to *create* content then the issue of "where the industry is headed" is irrelevant.

Where is YOUR business headed online?

Unless you are a street vendor who relies on walk-by traffic for 99.9% of your sales, there is a probably a pretty compelling reason for you to have an online presence.

Do you want to stay in business? Do you want more business? Then you need to be producing content that tells the people with whom you want to do business what you do and how you do it.

The digital revolution may sound like a techie thing that relies on data, analytics, IT and coding.

But when you strip all that stuff away, it is actually, at its heart, about finding the people your business is here to serve and starting conversations with them that might lead to a sale.

Content marketing is about people. Just like your business.

Quotes about Content Marketing:

Source: http://www.exacttarget.com/blog/content-marketing-experts/

You must market your marketing. ~ *Jay Baer, Convince and Convert*

Make the prospect a more informed buyer with content. ~ *Robert Simon, Four Seasons Hotels*

Content isn't King, it's the Kingdom. ~ *Lee Odden, TopRank Marketing*

Content is anything that adds value to the reader's life. ~ *Avinash Kaushik, Google*

Your goal should be to own quality time in your customer's inbox. ~ *Drew Davis, Brandscaping*

Content marketing is all about telling a compelling story. ~ *Joe Pulizzi, Content Marketing Institute*

The best marketing doesn't feel like marketing. ~ *Tom Fishburne, Marketoonist*

Attract. Engage. Convert. ~ *Lee Odden, TopRank Marketing*

Content: there is no easy button. ~ *Scott Abel, Content Strategist*

Be the best answer. ~ *Lee Odden, TopRank Marketing*

Good content is not storytelling. It's telling your story well. ~ *Ann Handley, MarketingProfs*

Content should ask people to do something and reward them for it. ~ *Lee Odden, TopRank Marketing*

The mantra should change from "Always Be Closing" to "Always He Helping." ~ *David Hahn, LinkedIn*
Source: http://www.toprankblog.com/2014/12/content-marketing-influencers/
Michael Brenner   @BrennerMichael

"Content is the atomic particle of all marketing across paid, owned, and earned channels. A Culture of Content starts with an obsession of customer."

Content Marketing Best Practices Report: Creating a Culture of Content / Ann Handley   @annhandley

"Does your content lead readers on a journey, or does it merely stuff them as leads into a pipeline?" Infographic: How to Grow Your Audience – 10 Tips from Facebook, MarketingProfs, ExactTarget, Copyblogger

 Joe Pulizzi   @JoePulizzi

"If we only talk about ourselves, we'll never reach customers"
5 Content Marketing Best Practices Most Businesses Aren't Doing, but Should! #SMMW14
 Mark Schaefer   @markwschaefer

"Are you human? Isn't that the essence of how this online world started, why we love social media, and what people expect if you are going to build trust and loyalty? And yet, this is getting increasingly lost in a world preoccupied with traffic, search rankings and automated marketing software."
5 Must Read Perspectives on Social Media Marketing Strategy
 Scott Stratten   @unmarketing

"I'm the first person to preach about customer experience, but if your product is terrible, I don't care if you're the greatest customer/community believer in the world, it won't help. We always talk about the importance of social media, of being where the customer conversation is, but we need to tend to our own home first."

Content Marketing Tactics

Brian Clark   @brianclark

"To please your audience, research their problems & desires, observe their content interactions & iterate." Infographic: How to Grow Your Audience – 10 Tips from Facebook, MarketingProfs, ExactTarget, Copyblogger

Jason Miller (client)   @JasonMillerCA

"Take your content and treat it like leftover turkey. Slice and dice it and use it in as many ways possible." 18 More Amazing Search & Digital Marketing Takeaways from #MNSummit

Ann Handley   @annhandley

"Writing doesn't have to be long to be meaningful. I'd argue that the words we use everywhere – on our websites, on our landing pages, on our LinkedIn profiles and so on – are just as important as the words we use in places we typically think of as 'writing.' "
Everybody Writes: Your Go-To Guide to Creating Ridiculously Good Content – Interview with Ann Handley
Michael Stelzner   @Mike_Stelzner

"Those that pitch are becoming ignored. A little bit of selling here and there is great, but those marketers who do nothing but sell, sell, sell, are gonna get ignored, dismissed and overlooked by consumers and prospects. Get cracking folks, it's time to actually care. That means dedicating more resources to things that are harder to track, like answering customer questions and providing more value online."
21 Digital Marketing Trends & Predictions for 2015

Amy Higgins (client)   @amywhiggins

"When crafting a blog post, think about the title – if just the title is shared in a tweet, will someone want to read it?" Content Plus Social is A Sweet Song to Sing – Interview with Amy Higgins of Concur

Content Marketing Predictions

David Meerman Scott   @dmscott

"Marketing (one to many) and sales (one to one) are beginning to use the same techniques of content creation and real-time engagement. The best organizations will not run marketing and sales as separate "departments" but will merge the two functions into one customer facing organization focused on revenue generation."
21 Digital Marketing Trends & Predictions for 2015

Content Marketing ROI

Michael Brenner   @BrennerMichael

"Content Marketing ROI is no harder than ROI for the rest of marketing. But many folks ask the question more as a defense mechanism for change. You will hear marketers ask this question despite not knowing what the ROI is on the rest of their marketing spend. So start with that benchmark. What is the ROI of marketing? Content marketing ROI is easier because content marketing results are easier than something like advertising."

Lessons on Marketing Strategy and Content Marketing ROI – Michael Brenner Interview

Mark Schaefer   @markwschaefer

"The way I measure content marketing success would vary by every customer. I would start with this question — 'What is the behavior or attitude we are trying to change?' Usually we can backward engineer from that response to find a set of measurements or leading indicators to determine our progress."
A Practical Approach to Content Marketing Success – Interview with Mark Schaefer

Statistics:

From:
http://www.inboundmarketingagents.com/inbound-marketing-agents-blog/bid/279437/55-Shareable-Stats-on-Content-Marketing-Trends-and-Tactics
and
http://blog.hubspot.com/blog/tabid/6307/bid/11414/12-Mind-Blowing-Statistics-Every-Marketer-Should-Know.aspx:

78% of Internet users conduct product research online.
That means your website stands a good chance of being a prospect's "first impression." That also means your new business card isn't a business card—it's Google.

40% of US Smartphone owners compare prices on their mobile device while in-store, shopping for an item.
Is your business website optimized for mobile devices ? If not, you may be missing out on hundreds of sales opportunities.

200 Million Americans have registered on the FTC's "Do Not Call" list.

84% of 25-34 year-olds has left a favorite website because of intrusive or irrelevant advertising.
Frankly, I'm surprised this stat doesn't read "100%" and apply to a much wider age range.

57% of businesses have acquired a customer through their company blog.
Finally, some good news! Blogging is good. Intrusive ads are bad. See how simple it is?

41% of B2B companies and 67% of B2C companies have acquired a customer through Facebook.
If this stat doesn't poke a hole in the "Facebook is not useful for B2B companies" myth, I don't know what will.

The number of marketers who say Facebook is "critical" or "important" to their business has increased 83% in just 2 years.
That's right — *critical or important*. When a channel generates not only leads, but real revenue, you can't call it "experimental" any longer.

Companies that blog get 55% more web traffic.
The more you blog, the more pages Google has to index, and the more inbound links you're likely to have. The more pages and inbound links you have, the higher you rank on search engines like Google—thus the greater amount of traffic to your website. Which is why we repeat: *Blogging is good.*

Inbound marketing costs 62% less per lead than traditional, outbound marketing.
That's right— *62% less*. The average outbound lead costs $373. The average inbound lead costs $143. And as we love to say around here, "if it don't make dollars, it don't make sense." Outbound marketing *just don't make sense anymore.*

Nine in 10 organizations market with content.
(Source: Content Marketing Institute)

According to 37% of marketing managers, the most important way to engage customers is content-led websites. (Source: The CMA)

78% of chief marketing officers think custom content is the future of marketing. (Source: Hanley-Wood Business Media)

Eight out of 10 CMOs believe custom content should be an integral part of a marketing strategy.(Source: Hanley-Wood Business Media)

The use of video content has risen from 52% in 2011 to 70% in 2012. (Source: Content Marketing Institute and Marketing Profs)

Companies with fewer than 10 employees typically allocate 42% of their marketing budget to content. (Source: Content Marketing Institute and Marketing Profs)

Companies with over 1,000 employees typically allocate 24% of their marketing budget to content. (Source: Content Marketing Institute and Marketing Profs)

Lack of human resources (42%) and lack of budget (35%) are key barriers to content marketing. (Source: eConsultancy and Outbrain)

54% of brands don't have an on-site, dedicated content creator. (Source: eConsultancy and Outbrain)

Creating original content is seen as the biggest challenge for 69% of content marketers. (Source:Curata)

Blogs

37% of marketers say blogs are the most valuable type of content marketing.(Source: Content Plus)

Companies with 10,000 or more employees use an average of 18 different content marketing tactics. (Source: Content Marketing Institute and Marketing Profs)

Company blogs are viewed as the "most useful" form of content.(Source: HubSpot)

79% of content marketers produce articles. (Source: Smart Insights)

The average marketer made 145 website content updates in 2012. (Source: Custom Content Council)

The ROI of Content

Content marketers use unique visitors (88%), pageviews per visitor (76%) and total pageviews (71%) as their main metrics. (Source: Econsultancy and Outbrain)

Companies that spend more than 50% of their lead generation budget on inbound marketing report a significantly lower cost-per-lead. (Source: Hubspot)

B2B companies that blog generate 67% more leads per month than those who do not blog. (Source:Social Media B2B)

Organic search leads have a 14.6% close rate, while outbound marketing leads have a 1.7% close rate (Source: Hubspot)

Articles with images get 94% more views. (Source: Jeff Bullas)

Image-based stories on Facebook get 37% more engagement. (Source: Jeff Bullas)

Sites can double their organic search traffic by including a video thumbnail in search rankings. (Source: Visibility IQ)

58% of consumers trust editorial content. (Source: Nielsen)

B2B Content Marketing

91% of B2B marketers use content marketing. (Source: Content Marketing Institute)

The average B2B marketer uses 12 different content marketing tactics. (Source: Content Marketing Institute and Marketing Profs)

11% of B2B companies use over 20 different content marketing tactics. (Source: Content Marketing Institute and Marketing Profs)

87% of B2B marketers use social media to distribute content, up from 74% in 2011. (Source: Content Marketing Institute and Marketing Profs)

79% of B2B marketers use content marketing to achieve brand awareness goals. (Source: Content Marketing Institute and Marketing Profs)

60% of B2B marketers use web traffic to measure effectiveness of content marketing. (Source: Content Marketing Institute and Marketing Profs)

54% of brands cited increased engagement as the number one value of content. (Source: Econsultancy and Outbrain)

74% of European online retailers believe they can influence what consumers buy. (Source: Intershop)

Only 38% of brands have a defined a content marketing strategy. (Source: Econsultancy and Outbrain)

23% use a cross-departmental approach to content marketing. (Source: Econsultancy and Outbrain)

28% of B2B companies use 5-9 different content marketing tactics. (Source: Content Marketing Institute and Marketing Profs)

B2C Content Marketing
86% of B2C marketers use content marketing. (Source: Content Marketing Institute)

Consumer Insights
80% of business decision-makers prefer to get company information in a series of articles versus an advertisement. (Source: Content Marketing Institute)

60% of consumers are more likely to be on the lookout for products when looking at content marketing. (Source: The CMA)

68% of consumers are likely to spend time reading content from a brand they are interested in. (Source: The CMA)

82% of consumers like reading content from brands when it's relevant. (Source: The CMA)
70% of consumers prefer getting to know a company via articles rather than ads. (Source: Content Plus)

70% of consumers say content marketing makes them feel closer to the sponsoring company. (Source: Content Marketing Institute)

60% of consumers feel more positive about a company after reading custom content on its site. (Source: Content Plus)

90% of consumers find custom content useful, and 78% believe that organizations behind the content are interested in building good relationships. (Source: TMG Custom Media)

About the Author

Susan Crossman is a veteran writer who has spent decades wielding the power tool of language to benefit businesses and individuals in search of greater success and consistent results. Via her content marketing company, Crossman Communications (www.crossmancommunications.com), Susan and her team create high quality online content that helps businesses connects with their target audience, explain their business proposition, differentiate them in a competitive market and motivate their ideal customers to take action.

An enthusiastic supporter of writing with clarity, she is the traditionally published author of four books: a novel (*Shades of Teale*), a collection of short stories (*Passages to Epiphany*), a writer's companion to help people write with more impact (*The Write Way*), and a book that explains the mysteries of content marketing (*Content Marketing Made Easy — Why You Need It / How To Do It*).

Aside from being an enthusiastic writer and business person, Susan is a traveller, a dreamer, a fan of classic rock and a lifelong learner.

If you'd like to know more about how she and her team can help you meet your business goals you're invited to:
- Connect with her on LinkedIn
- Follow her on Twitter (@CrossmanCom)
- Like the Crossman Communications Facebook page
- Add her to your circles on Google+ or
- Contact Susan directly at:

  susan@crossmancommunications.com.

Manor House
905-648-2193

www.ingramcontent.com/pod-product-compliance
Lightning Source LLC
Chambersburg PA
CBHW030239090526
44586CB00034B/216